On World Peace

Kabbalah Publishing is a registered DBA of
The Kabbalah Centre International, Inc.

For further information:

The Kabbalah Centre
155 E. 48th St., New York, NY 10017
1062 S. Robertson Blvd., Los Angeles, CA 90035

1.800.Kabbalah www.kabbalah.com

First Edition, July 2012

Printed in USA

ISBN: 978-1-57189-871-5

Design: HL Design (Hyun Min Lee) www.hldesignco.com

ON WORLD PEACE

KABBALAH PUBLISHING

Two Essays by the Holy Kabbalist Rav Yehuda Ashlag

Rav Yehuda Ashlag

EDITED BY MICHAEL BERG

Table of Contents

PART TWO: ONE PRECEPT

Acknowledgment

I would like to thank Meir Yeshurun for all of his help and diligence in preparing these writings for print.

Foreword

It is an exceedingly joyous occasion to be able to share with you this book. Over the past couple of years we have been researching, collecting and preparing for print many of the unpublished works of our teacher and Kabbalah Centre founder Rav Yehuda Ashlag.

The author of these works, the holy Kabbalist Rav Yehuda Ashlag of blessed memory, was the greatest kabbalist of our time and one of the most advanced thinkers as well. Unlike many who came before him who might have been akin to him in scholarship, wisdom, and holiness, Rav Ashlag was a revolutionary. What separates Rav Ashlag from other spiritual giants is that he knew that the ultimate purpose of this wisdom, and truly of all wisdoms, was not to simply learn and become enlightened. He knew that the ultimate purpose of true wisdom was to change our world and to create a new world and a new reality.

The true kabbalist knows with certainty that the world as we know it and have known it for thousands of years, a world filled with pain suffering and death, must change. This is not how life and our existence are meant to remain. Having the conviction and certainty in this understanding they do everything they can to study, write, teach and disseminate this understanding to as many people as possible. Through this work they know they can bring about the new world that we are meant to live in—a world with no pain, no suffering, no wars, and no death.

The two articles in this book are part of that work. Rav Ashlag develops and shares some of the most important teachings the world needs to hear and understand in order to create lasting peace and real change.

As you read this book I hope you are inspired to do as much as you can, much more then we have done so far to bring about this change in the world.

It is important to know that even before we do a single action to bring about real change and true world peace, our thoughts and consciousness about these most important of topics must change. It is also inspiring to realize that consciousness on its own creates change. My father and teacher Rav Berg would often remind us that "consciousness is everything," and as we change our consciousness about these important topics we are actually beginning to create change in our world.

We can and must in our lifetime bring about this change. It is my desire and prayer that this book brings us all closer to creating this change and experiencing true personal and global peace.

Blessings,

Michael

Part One

World Peace

פרק ראשון

שלום העולם

World Peace

Mercy and Truth have met,
Righteousness and Peace have kissed.
Truth will rise up from Earth,
and Righteousness looks upon from Heaven.
And the Creator will give goodness
and our land will yield its crops.
(Psalms 85: 11-13)

Everything in Reality Has the Right to Exist

Everything that exists in reality, whether good or bad—including even the most evil and damage-causing thing in the world—has the right to exist, to the degree that destroying it and removing it completely from the world is forbidden. Rather, our duty is to only repair or fix it and to guide it towards goodness, for even a casual observation of any sort at the work of Creation that lies before us is enough [for us] to infer the high degree of perfection of Him Who has created it.

Therefore, we have to understand and to take great care that we do not find faults in any part of Creation, declaring [this part or that] to be superfluous and unnecessary, because this amounts to giving a bad name, heaven forbid, to Him Who created it.

It is widely known that during the days of Creation, the Creator did not complete His Creation. This is why we find that each and every part of reality, both in general and in its particulars, is subject to the laws of gradual evolution, from a state of complete absence all the way to the point of its maximum growth.

בקורת לשלום העולם

חסד ואמת נפגשו,
צדק ושלום נשקו,
אמת מארץ תצמח
וצדק משמים נשקף.
גם ה' יתן הטוב,
וארצינו תתן יבולה.
(תהלים פ"ה י"א)

כל דבר שישנו במציאות יש לו זכות קיום

כל דבר שישנו בהמציאות, הן טוב והן רע, ואפילו היותר רע ומזיק שבעולם, יש לו זכות קיום, במדה, שאסור להשחיתו ולבערו כליל מהעולם, אלא שמוטל עלינו רק לתקנו ולהביאו למוטב, שהרי מתוך הסתכלות כל שהיא במלאכת הבריאה שלפנינו, די לנו להחליט על גודל מדת שלימותו של הפועל אותה.

ולכן עלינו להבין להזהר מלהטיל דופי בשום פרט מהבריאה לומר שמיותר הוא ואין בו צורך, שיש בזה משום הוצאת שם רע ח"ו חס ושלום על הפועל שלה.

אמנם דבר זה ידוע לכל, שהבורא ית' יתברך לא השלים את הבריאה בעת שבראה כי כן אנו מוצאים בכל פנה ופנה מהמציאות שלפנינו, והן בכללותה והן בפרטיותה, נתונה היא תחת חוקים של התפתחות הדרגתי, החל מן ההעדר עד גמר גידולו.

This is the reason why, for example, when we taste the bitterness of a fruit in its initial stages of growth, we do not judge this to be a [lit. as an existence of] fault or blemish in the fruit. We all know the reason for the bitter taste: It is because the fruit has not yet completed its [growth or] process of evolution all the way to the ultimate end.

This, too, is the case with all other particular parts of reality. Thus, if we feel that some particular part of Creation is destructive or evil, this indicates only that it is in a transition phase in terms of its evolutional process. In any case, we should not conclude that it is not good and find faults in this particular part, for this would be unwise.

ומטעם זה, אם למשל אנו טועמים טעם מר בפירי בתחילת גידולה, אין הדבר נידון אצלינו כמציאות מום ודופי בהפירי, משום, שכולנו יודעים את הסבה, שהוא משום שהפירי הזו עדיין לא גמרה את תהליך ההתפתחות שלה עד לקצה.

וכזה הוא המקרה ביתר הפרטים של המציאות, אם אך מרגישים בחינת רע והזק באיזה פרט, הנה זה רק מעיד על עצמו, שנמצא עדיין במצב של מדרגת מעבר מן תהליך ההתפתחותי שלו, ובכל אופן אין לנו לקבוע ולהחליט כי ברע הוא ולהטיל דופי בפרט הזה, כי לא מחכמה הוא.

False World Reformers

This is the source of all the weaknesses of world reformers throughout history: They have looked upon human beings as if they were improperly functioning machines that need repair, that is, the broken parts must be removed and replaced with properly corrected ones. This is the sole purpose of these world reformers: to exterminate all that is bad and destructive in the human species.

And, in fact, had not the Creator Himself stood up against them, surely they would have succeeded long ago in sifting the human being as if through a sieve and leaving in him only that which is good and beneficial. But the Creator guards all aspects of His Creation with great care and does not let anyone destroy anything that is in His possession: He only allows [these "reformers"] to put [a person] right [lit. restore him] and transform him to good, as explained above.

Therefore, all these false world reformers would vanish from the face of the Earth, while the evil qualities of the world would not be removed from the face of the Earth; rather, they [the evil qualities] are waiting and counting the number of levels of evolution that they need to go through until they have evolved to the highest level [lit. reach a complete ripening process].

By this point, those very same evil qualities will have transformed and become good and beneficial, as the Creator had originally conceived of them. This is like a fruit sitting on the branch of a tree, waiting and counting the days and months that it must go through until its ripening process is completed; when its taste and sweetness will be revealed to everyone.

מתקני העולם המדומים

ומכאן כל החולשות למתקני העולם שבהדורות, כי המה רואים את האדם כמו מכונה שאינה עובדת כראוי, שצריכים לתקנה, דהיינו להסיר ממנה את החלקים המקולקלים להחליפם באחרים המתוקנים. כן כל מגמתם של המתקני עולם הללו, רק לבער את כל רע וכל מזיק שבמין האדם.

ואמת הוא, שלולא הבורא ית' בעצמו עמד לנגדם, ודאי שהיו כבר מספיקים מזמן לנפות את האדם כבכברה, ולהותיר בו רק טוב ומועיל בלבד. אלא, מתוך שהבורא ית' שומר על כל הפרטים שבהבריאה שלו בהקפדה יתירה, ואינו מרשה למי שהוא, להשחית שום דבר שברשותו, אלא רק להחזירו ולהפכו למוטב בלבד, כדברינו לעיל.

לפיכך כל המתקנים ממין האמור יתמו מהארץ, והמדות הרעות שבעולם לא יתמו מהארץ, אלא שמחכים ומונים את מספר המדרגות של התפתחות המחויבים עוד לעבור עליהם, עד שיבואו לגמר בישולם.

אשר אז אותם המדות רעות בעצמן מתהפכות ונעשות למדות טובות ומועילות, כמו שחשב עליהם הבורא ית' מראש. בדומה לפירי היושבת לה על ענפי העץ, ומחכה וסופרת לה הימים והחדשים המחויבים עוד לעבור עליה, עד שתגמור בישולה, שיתגלה אז טעמה ומתיקותה לכל אדם.

Governance of Heaven and Governance of the Earth

Of course, one must know that the said law of evolution, which applies to all reality and which promises to transform anything that is not good into something good and beneficial, is able to act by the power of the governance of Heaven Above, that is, without consulting with humans who dwell on Earth.

On the other hand, the Creator has indeed bestowed wisdom and governance upon humans and has enabled them to take the said law of evolution under their own authority and governance, and in doing so allows one to greatly accelerate this process of evolution, according to his will and in complete freedom and independence, with respect to the limitation of time.

Thus, there are two [forms of] Governance that act in accordance with this evolution. One is the Governance of Heaven, which assures the transformation of everything that is bad and destructive into being good and beneficial, although this procedure, by its nature, takes time and moves extremely slowly and sluggishly. And if what is evolving is a sentient, live being, the result is that it suffers horrible pains and anguish while it lies under the compression of evolution, which moves with immense cruelty.

On the other hand, there is the Governance of the Earth, which means human beings, who have assumed governance over the laws of evolution. These people are powerful enough to free themselves from the fetters of time, and in so doing, they are hastening the End—which means, the end of the process of ripening and correction, which is the end of its development.

And this is in accord with what our sages said (*Talmud*, Tractate *Sanhedrin*, 98a) about the end of the process of salvation and redemption for the Israelites. Commenting upon the quote: "I am the Lord; in its time, I shall hasten it," they said, "If they merit it, I will hasten it; if they don't merit it, it will be in its time." (Isaiah 60:22)

ממשלת השמים וממשלת הארץ

אמנם יש לדעת, שחוק התפתחות האמור השפוך על כל המציאות המבטיח להחזיר כל רע לטוב ומועיל, הנה הוא פועל את כל פעולותיו בכח ממשלת השמים ממעל, כלומר, מבלי שאלת פיהם של בני האדם יושבי הארץ.

ולעומת זה, אמנם, שכל וממשלה נתן השי"ת בהאדם, והרשהו לקבל את חוק ההתפתחות האמור, תחת רשותו וממשלתו עצמו, אשר אז נמצא בזה שממהר מאד את הפרוצדורא תהליך הזאת של ההתפתחות, לפי חפצו, באופן חפשי ובלתי תלוי לגמרי בכבלי הזמן.

באופן, שיש כאן ב' ממשלות הפועלות בדרכי התפתחות האמורה: אחת היא ממשלת השמים, המבטחת לעצמה להחזיר כל רע ומזיק לטוב ומועיל, אלא שבא בעתו כדרכו בכבדות ובאריכת הזמן. ואם הדבר המתפתח הוא בעל חי ומרגיש, נמצא שסובל כאבים ויסורין נוראים, בזמן שמונח תחת מכבש ההתפתחות, העושה דרכיו באכזריות רבה.

ולעומת זה יש ממשלת הארץ דהיינו בני אדם, שלקחו את חוקי ההתפתחות האמור, תחת ממשלתם עצמם, שכחם יפה, להשתחרר לגמרי מכבלי הזמן, ונמצאים ממהרים מאד את הקץ, כלומר, את גמר בישולו ותיקונו של הדבר, שהוא הקץ של ההתפתחות שלו.

וכדברים האלה אמרו חכמינו ז"ל, (בסנהדרין [דף] צ"ח עמוד ע"א) על גמר גאולתם וגמר תיקונם של ישראל, שביארו הכתוב (ישעיהו ס', כב'), אני ה' בעתה אחישנה: זכו -אחישנה, לא זכו - בעתה.

Liberated from the Fetters of Time

They wish to say [here] that if the Israelites merit and adopt the law of evolution—through which they will transform their bad qualities into good ones—and bring [evolution] under their own governance, which means that they will focus their hearts and their minds on correcting their bad qualities and transforming them into good ones, then "I [the Creator] shall hasten it."

That means that the Israelites would thereby be completely liberated from the fetters of time. But this End is entirely dependent upon their own desire, which means that it is a function of the majority of their actions and attention. In this [way], they would be found to be "hastening" the End. But [even] if they did not merit taking the evolution of their bad qualities under their own governance, but instead chose to leave it in the hands of the Governance of Heaven, they are still [lit. even then] guaranteed the completion of their salvation and the completion of their correction.

[This is] because they have [lit. there is] complete trust in the Governance of Heaven, which operates according to the law of gradual evolution, [correcting] level after level, until it transforms all that is evil and destructive into good and beneficial, just like the fruit on the tree. And the End is sure, except that it will come "in its time." This means that the matter is completely dependent upon and connected to the dimension of time because this gradual development must pass through many levels of various kinds until it reaches its End. The nature of this process is to proceed very slowly and with great sluggishness and ends up taking a very long time indeed.

What emerges out of what we have discussed thus far is that what is evolving is a living sentient being, who must, in the course of passing through these evolutionary stages, undergo great and terrible suffering. This is because the driving force inherent in each level [lit. these levels]—a force that is able to push a human being from a lower level to a higher one—is powerful simply because it uses the propelling energy of the suffering and pain that have

משוחררים מכבלי הזמן

רצונם לומר, שאם יזכו ישראל ויקחו את חוק התפתחות, הצריך לעבור על מדותיהם הרעות עד שיתהפכו לטובות, ויביאו אותו תחת ממשלתם עצמם, דהיינו שישימו לבם ודעתם לתקן בעצמם את כל המדות הרעות שבהם, ולהפך אותם למדות טובות, אז "אחישנה".

כלומר, שנמצאים משוחררים לגמרי מכבלי הזמן, אלא הקץ הזה תלוי מעתה בחפצם עצמם, דהיינו רק לפי רוב המעשה והתשומת לב, ונמצאים בזה ש"מחישים" את הקץ. אבל אם לא זכו לקבל את התפתחות מדותיהם הרעות תחת ממשלתם עצמם, אלא יעזבוהו תחת ממשלת השמים, הנה גם אז, מובטחים בגמר גאולתם ובגמר תיקונם.

כי יש בטחון מלא בממשלת השמים, הפועלת על פי חוק ההתפתחות הדרגתי, מדרגה אחר מדרגה, עד שמהפכת כל רע ומזיק לטוב ומועיל, כמו הפירי על העץ, והקץ בטוח לגמרי אלא "בעתה". כלומר, שכבר הדבר תלוי ומקושר לגמרי במדת הזמן, כי התפתחות הדרגתי הזה עד ביאתו להקץ, הנה מוכרח לעבור עליו מדרגות שונות ומרובות, שדרכם לבא בכבדות ובאטיות גדולה וארוכה ביותר עד שלוקחים זמן מרובה מאד.

ומתוך שבנידון לפנינו, הרי דבר המתפתח הם בעלי חיים ומרגישים, הנה מוכרחים ג"כ גם כן לקבל במצבי התפתחות הללו, יסורין גדולים ונוראים ביותר, משום שכל הכח הדוחף שישנו במדרגות הללו, עד כדי להעלות האדם ממדרגה נמוכה למדרגה מעולה ממנה,

accumulated in the lower level. Only when this [pain and suffering] have become unbearable is one forced to relinquish that level and ascend to a more important one.

The sages said: "The Creator installs a king for them whose decrees are as hard as those of Haman[1]. Then the Israelites do *teshuvah* [repentance], whereupon He brings them back to the good [path]." (*Talmud*, Tractate *Sanhedrin*, 97b) And the End that is promised to the Israelites, according to the law of gradual evolution, is referred to as "in its time," which means bound by the fetters of time. And the sure End for the Israelites, if they take the evolution of their own qualities into their own hands, is called "I shall hasten it," i.e., it is completely independent of time.

1. An advisor to the Persian king (520 BCE), who decreed the extermination of all Israelites living in 127 countries under the rule of the Persian Empire.

אינו יותר, רק מסבת כח דחיפה של יסורין ומכאובים, שנתקבצו בהמדרגה הנמוכה עד שאי אפשר עוד לסבול, אשר אז מוכרחים לעזוב אותה, ולעלות למדרגה חשובה ממנה.

ועל דרך שאמרו חז"ל (מסכת סנהדרין צ"ז ע"ב) "אלא הקב"ה מעמיד להן מלך שגזירותיו קשות כהמן, וישראל עושין תשובה ומחזירן למוטב". והנה הקץ המובטח לבא לישראל על פי חוק ההתפתחות הדרגתי הנזכר, מכונה "בעתה", כלומר, הקשור בעבותות הזמן. והקץ הבטוח לישראל, על ידי שיקחו את התפתחות מדותיהם תחת ידיהם עצמם, מכונה "אחישנה", כלומר, בלתי תלוי לגמרי בזמן.

Absolute Good and Not Good (Evil)

But before we start contemplating the correction of that which is not good in the human species, we have to first establish the value of these abstract terms: "Good and Not Good (Evil)." That is, what is our standard against which we evaluate the quality and the deed when we determine whether it is a good and beneficial quality or deed, or on the contrary, whether it is the opposite: a not-good quality or deed.

In order to understand this, we need to know well the relationship [lit. relative value] between the individual and the collective, that is, between an individual and his community in which he lives and out of which he is nourished, materially as well as spiritually. And from actual reality, we learn that the individual could not exist, if he would isolate himself without a community efficient enough to serve him and to help him fulfill his needs.

הטוב והרע האבסולוטי

ובטרם שאנו נכנסים בהתבוננות של תיקון הרע שבמין האנושי, צריכים לקבוע מקודם את ערכם של אותם השמות המופשטות "טוב ורע", כלומר, כלפי מי מעריכים את המדה ואת המעשה, עד להגדיר, אם מדה ומעשה טוב הוא, או להיפך שהוא מדה ומעשה רע?

ולהבין זה, צריכים לידע הטב את הערך היחסי שבין הפרט והכלל, דהיינו בין היחיד אל הצבור שלו, שהיחיד חי מתוכו וניזון מתוכו הן בחומריות והן ברוחניות. ומן המציאות הממשית אנו למדים, שאין כלל זכות קיום להיחיד, אם היה מבודד לעצמו בלי ציבור מספיק, שישרתוהו ויעזרוהו בסיפוק צרכיו.

Humans were Created to Live a Sociable Life

From this, we understand that, to begin with, the human being was created to live a life of society, and each and every individual in society is like a cog that is tied together to a number of other cogs, all of which are interdependent and conditioned by one machine. The individual cog has no freedom of motion in and of itself; rather, it is pulled into motion by the movement of all the cogs in a pre-set direction, which serves to make the machine more capable of fulfilling its general function. And if one cog malfunctions, this malfunction is not evaluated and examined with regard to that cog in and of itself, but rather according to its function and the service that it provides to the whole machine.

In the same manner, we have to evaluate the degree of Goodness of each individual in his community, not according to how Good that individual is in himself, but by how much service he provides to the community as a whole. And likewise, we do not evaluate the degree of Evil of each individual, except with regard to the damage that he does to the general community, rather than according to his value in himself.

These things are as obvious as the sun at noon, in terms of both the truth and the Goodness inherent in them. The collective has only what is there in the individuals, and the Good of society means the Good of every individual in that society. And an individual who harms the society ends up taking his share of that harm. Likewise, an individual who benefits his society ends up having his share of that Goodness. This is because individuals exist only as parts of the collective, and the collective has no additional value or added importance beyond being the sum total of the individuals that compose it.

האדם נברא לחיות חיי חברה

ומבינים אנו מזה, שהאדם נברא מלכתחילה לחיות חיי חברה, וכל יחיד ויחיד שבהחברה, הוא כמו גלגל אחד המלוכד בגלגלים מספר, המותנים במכונה אחת. שהגלגל היחיד, אין לו חירות של תנועה בערך יחידותו לפי עצמו, אלא שנמשך עם תנועת כלל הגלגלים, בכוון ידוע, להכשיר את המכונה לתפקידה הכללי. ואם יארע איזה קלקול בגלגל, אין הקלקול נערך ונבחן כלפי יחידותו של הגלגל לפי עצמו, אלא שנערך לפי תפקידו ושירותו כלפי כללות המכונה.

והנה כמו כן יש לנו להעריך מדת טובו של כל יחיד ויחיד בתוך הצבור שלו, לא לפי טובת עצמו, אלא לפי שירותו את הצבור בכללו וכן להיפך, אין אנו מעריכים את מדת הרע של כל יחיד ויחיד, אלא לפי הערך שמזיק את הצבור הכללי, ולא לפי ערכו עצמו האינדיוידואלי.

והדברים הללו ברורים כשמש בצהרים, הן מצד האמת שבהם, והן מצד הטוב שבהם, כי אין בכלל אלא מה שבפרט, וטובת הצבור, פירושו, טובת כל יחיד ויחיד שבאותו הצבור, והיחיד המזיק להציבור, סופו, שנוטל גם חלקו בהזק הזה. וכן היחיד המטיב להצבור, נוטל חלקו בהטבה ההיא, להיות היחידים ההם רק חלקי הצבור, ואין בהצבור שום ערך כל שהוא והוספה משהו, יותר מסכום היחידים הללו שבו.

The Collective and the Individual Are One and the Same

For this reason, we need to understand that both the collective and the individuals are one and the same, and that no harm is caused to the individual because of his great subservience to the collective. That is because the freedom of the collective and the freedom of the individual are also one and the same because just as they share the Good between them, so, too, do they share freedom between them.

Thus, good qualities and bad qualities and good deeds and bad deeds are considered [lit. measured] as such only with reference to the Good of the whole. Naturally, these things are true [only] if all the individuals in the community perform their duties toward the collective perfectly and are compensated according to what they really deserve (in other words, no one takes a portion that belongs to his friend).

Indeed, if a small portion of a community does not behave in this manner, the end result is that not only do they harm the community, but they also harm themselves. While there should be no need to discuss in detail something that is familiar and known, we have discussed this at length in order to draw attention to the weak spot, that is, the place that needs to be corrected.

In other words, we wanted to show that the only thing lacking in this world is for each individual to understand that his own Good depends on the just service that he renders to the collective, as well as on the just allocation to every individual member of the collective. Certainly, we have a world of plenty, but we need to know how to enjoy it.

הצבור והיחידים היינו הך

ולפיכך יש להבין, שהצבור והיחידים היינו הך, ואין שום ריעותא להיחיד מחמת השעבוד הגדול אל הצבור, שאפילו חירות הצבור וחירות היחיד, ג'כ גם כן דבר אחד הם, כי כמו שמחלקים ביניהם את הטוב, כן מחלקים ביניהם את החירות.

הרי שמדות טובות ומדות רעות ומעשים טובים ומעשים רעים, נערכים רק כלפי טובת הצבור, וכמובן, אשר הדברים, אמורים דוקא, אם כל היחידים שבהצבור ממלאים את תפקידם להצבור בשלימות, וכן נוטלים הספקתם כפי המגיע להם באמת, כלומר, שלא יטול חלק חבירו.

אמנם אם מקצת הצבור אינם מתנהגים כאמור, הרי הפועל יוצא מזה, שלא לבד, שמזיקים להצבור, אלא שניזוקים גם בעצמם. ואין להאריך יותר בדבר ידוע ומפורסם, אלא, שהמשכנו הדברים עד כה, כדי להביא לפני העינים את נקודת התורפה, כלומר, אותו המקום התובע את תיקונו.

דהיינו, להראות, שאינו חסר בעולם יותר אלא רק שכל יחיד יבין את טובתו, התלוי בשרות הצודקת של כל יחיד להצבור ובחלוקה הצודקת לכל יחיד מהצבור. וזה ודאי שיש לנו עולם מלא מכל טוב אלא שצריכים לדעת איך להנות ממנה.

The Means for Correcting the World: Mercy, Truth, Righteousness, and Peace

Now we have properly verified the level of Goodness in its [true] image that is in store for us, that is to say: 1) that all the individuals in society fulfill their role perfectly, every one according to what was assigned to him, and 2) that each individual take his share of the available sustenance, at a just rate, in a way that will not touch his friend's share. From now on, we must see and reflect upon the actual ways and means that are at our disposal to hasten [achieving] for ourselves that goodness and happiness.

There are four qualities that are instrumental in [achieving] this, and they are Mercy, Truth, Righteousness, and Peace—the qualities that all world reformers have always used to this very day. More accurately, these are the four qualities with which the development of humanity, meaning the Governance of Heaven, has paved its gradual way, until it brought humanity to its present condition.

And we have already spoken about this earlier, that it would behoove and benefit us to take the law of evolution into our own hands and to assume governance ourselves. In this way, we will rid ourselves of all manner of suffering, which evolution [lit. the developmental history] has in store for us from here onwards. Therefore, we will look at and inquire into these four qualities to know well what they have given us to this present day, and in so doing, inform ourselves about what further assistance we can hope to obtain from [these qualities] in the future.

אמצעי תיקון העולם: חסד אמת צדק ושלום

ואחר שודענו היטב את מדת הטוב המקווה לנו, כצלמו ודמותו דהיינו הא׳, שכל היחידים שבהצבור ימלאו את תפקידם בשלימות, כל אחד את המוטל עליו. והב׳, שכל יחיד יטול את חלקו בהספקה, בשיעור צודק, באופן, שלא יגע אחד בחלק חבירו. הנה מעתה יש לנו לראות ולהתבונן, בהדברים והאמצעים שישנם ברשותינו למעשה, בכדי למהר לעצמינו את הטוב והאושר ההוא.

וארבע מדות נמצאים לנו לדבר זה, שהם: חסד, אמת, צדק, ושלום, שבהם שמשו כל מתקני העולם עד היום הזה, או יותר נכון, אשר בד׳ מדות הללו עשתה עד כאן ההתפתחות האנושית, דהיינו ממשלת השמים, את דרכה המדרגתי, עד שהביאה את האנושיות אל המצב של היום.

וכבר דברנו מזה לעיל, אשר יאות לנו ומוטב בעדינו, לקחת את חוק ההתפחות תחת ידינו וממשלתינו בעצמינו, כי אז נפטור את עצמינו מכל חומר היסורין, שההסטוריא ההתפתחותית רושמת בעדינו מכאן ולהבא, ולפיכך נראה ונפשפש בד׳ מדות הללו, לדעת היטב מה שנתנו לנו עד היום הזה, כדי לידע מתוכם, מה שיש לנו לקוות עוד להסתייע מהם להבא.

Truth: From Theory to Practice

Now in theory, there is no better quality than Truth. This is because all the Goodness that we have spoken of earlier, which occurs when every individual performs his duties to the collective and receives his rightful share, this is none other than Truth. But the problem is that, in fact, this quality is not accepted by the people of society. And this actual difficulty inherent in Truth proves that there is something wrong here, and will cause it not be accepted by society, and we need to inquire what it is.

And if we really examine the quality of Truth in terms of its practical potential, we will inevitably find it vague and very complicated, and beyond our ability to fathom its meaning [lit. the human eye to capture it]. After all, Truth demands that we treat all individuals in society as equals, so that each one of them receives a share according to his effort, neither less nor more. This is the sole basis for Truth, and one that should not be doubted, because it is obvious and certain that anyone who wants to benefit from the work of another is going against Truth and wisdom.

Indeed, how can we picture and look into this Truth in a way that will be acceptable to all members of society? For example, if we consider the matter according to the observed hourly work that an individual performs—that is, if each individual member of society should work an equal amount of hours—this still would not reveal the aforementioned Truth to us at all.

Moreover, there is an obvious lie here because of two things. The first is a physical issue: Because not everyone is naturally endowed with an equal capacity for work, we could have one member of society who, because of his weakness, gets more tired in one hour of work than his colleague who works two hours or more.

There is also a psychological issue here, because a very slow person by his nature gets much more tired in one hour than his friend does in two or more. If we consider all this from the perspective of

האמת: הלכה למעשה

והנה להלכה, ודאי שאין לנו מדה יותר טובה מהאמת, שהרי כל הטוב שגדרנו לעיל במילוא תפקידו של כל יחיד להצבור, ובנטילת חלק צודק לכל יחיד, הרי, אין דבר זה אלא דבר "אמת". אלא כל החסרון הוא, אשר למעשה, אין מדה זו מתקבלת כלל על הצבור. והנה הקושי הזה למעשה, שישנו בהאמת האמור מוכח מתוכו, שיש כאן איזה פגם וגורם שלא יתקבל על הצבור, וצריכים להתבונן בו מהו?

וכשתפשפש היטב בהאמת האמור, בכשרונו המעשי, תמצאהו בהכרח שהוא מעורפל ומסובך מאד, ואי אפשר כלל לעין האנושי לעמוד עליו. שהרי, האמת מחייב אותנו, להשוות כל היחידים שבהצבור, שיקבלו את חלקם לפי מדת יגיעתם, לא פחות ולא יותר. וזהו הבסיס היחידי האמיתי, שאין להרהר אחריו, שהרי ודאי הוא, שכל הרוצה להנות מיגיעתו של חבירו, הוא כנגד הדעת והאמת הברור האמור.

אמנם, כיצד יצוייר לנו לברר את האמת הזה, באופן שיתקבל על לב כל בני הצבור? למשל, אם נדון בדבר לפי העבודה הגלויה השעותית, שהיחיד עובד, דהיינו, שכל אחד מהצבור יעבוד מספר שעות מסוימות בשוה, אין זה עוד מגלה לנו כלל את האמת האמור.

ואדרבה, יש כאן שקר גלוי, משום ב' דברים: הא' הוא , ענין פיזי, כי אין הכח להעבודה מבחינת הטבע, שוה אצל כל אחד, ויש לך אחד מהחברה, שהוא מתיגע מפני חולשתו בשעה אחת, הרבה יותר מחבירו בשתי שעות או יותר.

וכן יש לפנינו ענין פסיכולוגי, כי העצל מאד מטבעו, מתיגע ג"כ גם כן בשעה אחת, יותר מחבירו בשתי שעות או יותר. לפי השקפת

the quality of clear Truth, we should not oblige one part of society to exert itself more than any other part as [individuals] attempt to satisfy their life's needs.

For, in fact, there are members of society who are naturally energetic and strong but who live off and benefit from the labor of others and maliciously take advantage of them. This is in direct opposition to Truth because such people exert themselves very little compared to the weak and slow in society.

And further, if we take into account the natural law of "following the majority," then this kind of Truth, which is based only on [lit. takes as its basis] manifested hourly labor, is not at all lasting because the weak and the slow always form the vast majority of people in a society, and they will not allow the minority of the energetic and the strong to take advantage of their [the weak and slow] effort and work.

And because the basis of the effort, which is where the clear Truth lies and where most of the people relate to, cannot be tested and evaluated at all, it follows that the quality of Truth is, in fact, unfit for being the criterion according to which the ways of the individual and the ways of society should be absolutely arranged, in a way that it would be completely satisfactory. [Truth] does not have the total fulfillment to be sufficient for regulating life at all, once the world has been brought to correction.

מדת האמת הברור אין לנו לחייב את חלק אחד להתייגע לספוק חייהם, יותר מלחלק השני שבחברה.

כי למעשה, נמצאים הגבורים והזריזים הטבעיים שבהחברה, שנהנים מיגיעתם של אחרים, ומנצלים אותם בזדון לבם, בהיפך מהאמת, כי הם מתייגעים מעט מאד לעומת החלשים והעצלים שבהחברה.

ואם נקח עוד בחשבון , את החוק הטבעי של אחרי רבים להטות, הרי מין אמת כזה, דהיינו לקבל לבסיס, רק את העבודה השעותית הגלויה, אינה כלל בן קיימא, כי החלשים והעצלים המה תמיד, הרוב הניכר שבין החברה, ולא ירשו להמיעוט הזריזים והגבורים שהמה ינצלו את כחם ויגיעתם.

ולפי שהבסיס של היגיעה, שעמו האמת הברור ועמו הרוב שבהחברה אינו ניתן לבדיקה ולהערכה כל עיקר נמצא מזה שמדת האמת אין לו שום כשרון למעשה לסדר על פיו את דרכי היחיד ודרכי הצבור באופן מוחלט, דהיינו שיניח את הדעת בהחלט, ואין בו כלל אותה הספקה הגמורה, המתאימה לסדרי החיים שבגמר התיקון של העולם.

Law of Unique Individuality

Moreover, there is an even greater problem here than the one mentioned earlier. There is no clearer Truth than the way of nature itself, and it is only natural that every individual feels himself the sole ruler in the world of the Creator and that everyone else was not created for any other purpose except to improve his life and to make it easier, to the point that he does not even feel any obligation to compensate the other.

Said simply, it is the nature of every human being to take advantage of all living beings for his own benefit, and whatever one [person] gives to another, he does out of necessity. Inherent in this necessity to give to another is, in fact, yet another form of taking advantage of the other, albeit in a very cunning manner and in a way that the other person will not feel it and will give [the thing] up of his own accord.

The reason for this is that the nature of any branch is to be close to its roots[2], and because the human soul is an extension of the Creator—Who is One, Only and Unique, and to Whom everything belongs—therefore the human, who is an extension of Him, feels that all the creatures of the world should be governed by him, for his own benefit.

This is an immutable law, but the difference [between individuals] is evident only in the type of choice that people make: One [person] chooses to take advantage of others by fulfilling his simple low desires; another tries to do so by achieving a position of power; and a third tries to do so by securing honor. To be sure, each of these [individuals] might have agreed to exploit the world in *all* these aspects—that is, in wealth, power, and honor—had it been possible for him to achieve [these goals] without much effort, but one must choose according to one's ability.

2. Both have the same qualities.

חוק היחודיות

ולא עוד, אלא שיש כאן, עוד צרה יותר גדולה מהאמור. כי אין לך אמת ברור ביותר, מדרך הטבע בעצמו, והנה טבעי הוא, שכל אדם ואדם מרגיש את עצמו בעולמו של הקב"ה הקדוש ברוך הוא כמו שליט יחיד, אשר כל זולתו לא נברא אלא להקיל ולשפר את חייו, עד מבלי להרגיש התחייבות כל שהוא מצדו, ליתן לו התמורה.

ובמלות פשוטות נאמר, שטבע כל אדם ואדם, לנצל את חיי כל הבריות שבעולם לטובת עצמו, וכל שנותן לזולתו אינו נותן אלא מחמת הכרח, אשר גם בהכרח הזה שנותן לו יש בו משום ניצול לזולתו, אלא בערמה רבה, באופן, שחבירו לא ירגיש זה, ויותר לו מדעתו.

וטעם הדבר הוא, מצד, שכל ענף טבעו קרוב לשורשו, ומתוך שנפשו של האדם נמשך מהש"ית מהשם יתברך, שהוא אחד יחיד והכל שלו, הנה כמו כן האדם הנמשך ממנו, מרגיש, שכל בריות העולם צריכים להמצא תחת ממשלתו, ולתועלתו הפרטי.

וזהו חוק ולא יעבור, אלא שההפרש בולט לעין רק במדת בחירתם של האנשים, שהאחד בחר לנצל את הבריות על ידי השגת תאוות נמוכות, והשני על ידי השגת ממשלה, והשלישי על ידי השגת כבוד, וכן אפילו כל אחד מהם, אם היה עלה לו הדבר בלו טורח מרובה, היה מסכים, גם לנצל העולם בכל אלו יחד, גם בעושר וגם בממשלה וגם בכבוד, אלא שמוכרח לבחור לפי אפשרותו.

This law may be called the Law of Unique Individuality within the hearts of humans. And no one is able to escape this law: The great are subject to it to a great degree, and the smaller ones to a smaller degree.

And this Law of Unique Individuality, which is inherent in the nature of everyone, should be neither condemned nor praised because it is a natural phenomenon. As such, it has as much right to exist as every other aspect of reality, and there is no chance that it will be eliminated from the world or even that it will be blurred in its expression, just as there is no chance that all of the human race will be removed from the face of the Earth. Therefore, we would not be lying if we said that this law is the "absolute truth."

Because it is undoubtedly so, how can we even try to appease the mind of an individual by promising to make him equal to all the other members of the community? After all, there is nothing more contrary to human nature than [equality], being that the sole purpose of the individual is to achieve a position higher than any other member of the community.

Thus, we have clearly demonstrated that based on the quality of truth, it is not realistic at all to establish good and accepted procedures for the life of the individual or the life of the community that would be satisfactory to, and completely agreed upon by, each and every individual—although this is what must be done to bring the process of correction to its completion.

וחוק הזה אפשר לכנותו, "חוק היחודיות" שבלב האדם, שאין כל אדם נמלט ממנו אלא הגדול לפי גדלו והקטן לפי קטנו.

והנה חוק היחודיות האמור שבטבע כל אדם, לא יגונה ולא ישובח, כי הוא מציאות טבעי, ויש לו זכות קיום כמו כל פרטי המציאות, ואין שום תקוה לבערו מהעולם או אפילו לטשטש צורתו במקצת, כמו שאין תקוה לבער את כל מין האדם מהארץ. ולפיכך לא נשקר כלל, אם נאמר על החוק הזה שהוא "האמת המוחלט".

ומאחר שכן הוא בלי ספק, איך נוכל כלל לנסות אפילו להניח הדעת של היחיד, בזה שנבטיח לו להשוותו במדה השוה, יחד עם כל בני הצבור, שאין לך דבר רחוק מהטבע אנושי יותר מזה, בשעה שכל מגמת היחיד הוא, להגביה על למעלה מכל בני הצבור כולו.

והנה הראינו היטב, שאין מציאות כלל להביא סדרים מאושרים וטובים לחיי היחיד ולחיי הצבור, על פי מדת האמת, באופן שיניחו את הדעת של כל יחיד ויחיד, שיתן עליהם את הסכמתו המוחלטת, כמו שצריך להיות לגמר התיקון.

People of Destruction and People of Construction

And now we will discuss the other three qualities, which are Mercy, Righteousness, and Peace. These [qualities] were seemingly created initially to be a support system to strengthen Truth, which has become very weak in our world. And you should know that this is the phase at which evolutionary history started its slow and gradual ascent up its levels of social order of the society's life.

In theory, all members of society agreed unequivocally not to deviate from their [mutually] agreed-upon Truth. However, what actually happened was that they all acted exactly contrary to Truth and to their agreement. Since then, Truth has fallen into the hands of the greatest liars and is never found among the weak and the righteous, who, therefore, cannot even be assisted by it to any degree whatsoever.

And because the quality of Truth could not be established as a way of life the number of members of the society who either were weak or taken advantage of became larger. This is the reason the qualities of Mercy and Righteousness appeared, so that they might act and support the social order. For society as a whole to exist, its more successful members had to support those who faltered [or fell] behind, so as not to harm society as a whole. Therefore, they [the successful] would treat them [the weak] leniently, that is to say, with Mercy and Righteousness.

Of course, the nature of these conditions would increase the number of those who falter and are being exploited, so much so that there are enough of them to protest against the successful ones and to initiate quarrels and squabbles; and this is the origin of the quality of Peace in the world. Hence, all these qualities—Mercy, Righteousness, and Peace—emerged from, and were born out of, the weakness of Truth.

בעלי החורבן ובעלי הבנין

ועתה ניקח את- ג' מדות הנשארים, שהם: חסד, צדק, ושלום. שלכאורה לא נבראו מתחילתם, אלא ליקח מהם סמוכין, להסמיך בהם את האמת החלש מאוד בעולמנו. ותדע, שמכאן התחילה ההסטוריא ההתפתחותית לטפס על דרגותיה האטיות והנחשלות, בהסידורים של חיי הצבור.

כי להלכה הסכימו כל בני החברה וקבלו עליהם בכל תוקף, לבלי לנטות מהאמת אף משהו. אמנם למעשה, כולם נהגו את עצמם בהיפך לגמרי והאמת המוסכם. ומאז, נפל גורלו של כל האמת בחלקם של השקרנים ביותר, ואינו מצוי לעולם אל החלשים והצדיקים, שיוכלו אפילו להסתייע מהאמת, לא מניה ולא מקצתיה.

והנה מתוך שלא יכלו להנהיג את מדת האמת בחיי הצבור, הנה נתרבו הנחלשים והנעשקים בתוך החברה, ומכאן יצאו ונצמחו מדת החסד והצדק, לפעול את פעולתם בסדרי החברה, כי כללות קיום החברה, היה מחייב את המוצלחים שבהם, לתמוך את הנחשלים, בכדי שלא להזיק את כללות החברה, ועל כן היו נוהגים עמהם לפנים משורת הדין, דהיינו, בחסד ובצדקה.

אמנם מטבע התנאים שכאלו, להרבות את הנחשלים והנעשקים, עד שמספיקים למחות בהמוצלחים ולעשות מריבות וקטטות, ומכאן יצא ונתגלה מדת השלום בעולם. הרי שכל אלו המדות חסד וצדקה ושלום, יצאו ונולדו מחולשת האמת.

And this is the reason that society was split into numerous factions. Some of them adopted Mercy and Righteousness, that is to say, giving up their possessions for the sake of others. Others clung to the quality of Truth, that is, Mine is Mine and Yours is Yours.

More simply, one could divide them into People of Construction and People of Destruction. People of Construction are interested in supporting and upholding the community as a whole. As a result they were often forced to give up their possessions for the sake of others.

But those who, by nature, were more inclined towards destruction and lawlessness were able to cling to the quality of Truth for their own benefit, believing that Mine is Mine and Yours is Yours, and never wanting to give up even a small part of their share for the sake of others. Being that they were, by nature, People of Destruction, they did not take into account that they were endangering the existence of the community.

והיא שגרמה להתפלגות החברה לכתות כתות: כי מהם תפסו להם את החסד והצדקה דהיינו, לותר מרכושו לאחרים. ומהם שתפסו להם את מדת האמת, דהיינו, שלי שלי ושלך שלך.

ובדברים יותר פשוטים, אפשר לחלקם, לבעלי בנין ולבעלי חורבן: כי בעלי הבנין, שהוא חפצים בבנינם ובטובתם של כללות הצבור, היו מוכרחים משום זה, לותר פעמים תכופים מרכושם לאחרים.

אבל אלו שהיו נוטים מטבעם לחורבן ולהפקרות, היו יכולים להתאחז במדת האמת לתועלתם הפרטי, דהיינו, שלי שלי ושלך שלך ולא היו רוצים לעולם, לותר אף משהו מחלקם לאחירים, מבלי לקחת בחשבון, שהמה מסכנים בזה את קיום הצבור, להיותם מטבעם בעלי חורבן.

Peacemakers

Only after these conditions created the greatest conflicts in society, endangering the existence of society as a whole, did peacemakers in society emerge who, by taking firmness and force into their own hands, revived the life of society. They did so by adopting what they believed were new and true conditions, which were meant to secure the existence of society in peace.

However, most of these peacemakers, who emerge and show up after every conflict, are naturally from the People of Destruction—that is, from those who seek Truth in the sense of Mine is Mine and Yours is Yours. The reason for this is that they are the powerful and courageous [individuals] in society and are referred to as heroes since they are always ready to sacrifice their own lives as well as the lives of society at large, if the society does not agree with their opinion.

Not so with the People of Construction in society, who are people of Mercy and Righteousness and who value both their own lives and the lives of other members of society as precious; thus they are not willing to endanger themselves or society [as a whole] just to force people to conform to their opinion.

For this reason, they are always the weaker aspect of society and are referred to as faint-hearted cowards. It is self-evident that the lawless brave ones will always be more victorious, and thus, it is only natural that all the peacemakers come from the People of Destruction and not from the People of Construction.

עושי השלום

ואחר שהתנאים האלו הביאו את החברה לקטטות גדולות ביותר, וכללות החברה באו לידי מצב של סכנה, הזה אז, צמחו ונתגלו עושי השלום בהחברה, שנטלו את התקיפות והכח שבידיהם, וחידשו את חיי החברה, על פי תנאים חדשים אמיתיים לפי דעתם, שיספיקו את קיום החברה בשלום.

אמנם עושי השלום האלו, הצומחים ובאים אחרי כל מחלוקת, הנה מצד טבע הדברים, באים ברובם, רק מבעלי החורבן, דהיינו ממבקשי האמת, מבחינת שלי שלי ושלך שלך, והוא, לטעם היותם בעלי הכח והאומץ שבהחברה, המכונים גבורים אמיצי הלב, מטעם שהמה המוכנים תמיד להפקיר את חיי עצמם ואת חיי כללות הצבור כולו, אם לא יסכימו הצבור לדעתם.

מה שאין כן בעלי הבנין שבהחברה, דהיינו בעלי החסד וצדקה, שיקר להם חיי עצמם וגם יקר להם חיי הצבור, אינם מוכנים להפקיר את עצמם והצבור ולהעמידם בסכנה, עד להכריח את הצבור להסכים לדעתם.

ולפיכך המה תמיד הצד החלש שבהחברה, המכונים מוגי הלב ופחדנים. ומובן מעצמו, שתמיד יד המופקרים אמיצי הלב על העליונה, שעל כן טבעי הוא הדבר, שכל עושי השלום מבעלי החורבן באים , ולא מבעלי הבנין.

Truth and Destruction Are One and the Same; Mercy and Construction Are One and the Same

We see from all this that any hope for Peace, which the people of our generation are desperately looking for, is useless, both from the point of view of the subject as well as from the point of view of the object. The subjects, who are the peacemakers of our generation and of every other generation and who have the power in their hands to make Peace in the world, are forever made from that human element known as People of Destruction. This is because they seek Truth, that is, they want the world to be run by the principle of Mine is Mine and Yours is Yours. So it is only natural that these are the people who aggressively push their views forward, to the point of endangering both their own lives and the lives of the entire society.

And this is what always gives them the power to overcome the other kind of human element—the People of Construction—who seek Mercy and Righteousness and who are willing to give their own [possessions] away for the sake of others in order to save the construction of the world; and they are the cowards who are faint of heart. In other words, seeking Truth is the same as destroying the world, and seeking Mercy is the same as the building the world. Therefore, one cannot hope that the People of Destruction will be those who will establish Peace.

And likewise, the Peace that all yearn for is also useless from the point of the object, that is to say, from the point of view of the conditions themselves of Peace. To this very day, it is not possible to create the conditions that are considered appropriate, according to the criterion of Truth, for both the life of the individual and the life of society, as desired by those peacemakers. It is inevitable that there has always been, and always will be, an important minority in society who will be unhappy with these conditions, just as we said earlier when we demonstrated the weakness of Truth, and these (people) will always be ready material for the new warmongers and for the new peacemakers, who will continue in this manner *ad infinitum.*

אמת וחורבן - היינו הך, חסד ובנין - היינו הך

ומהאמור אנו רואים, איך שתקוות השלום, שכל בני דורינו מחכים אליו בכליון עינים, הוא מחוסר ערך, הן מצד הנושא והן מצד הנשוא. כי הנושאים, דהיינו עושי השלום שבדורינו ובכל דור ודור, כלומר, אותם שהכח בידיהם לעשות שלום בעולם, הרי המה לעולם מאותו החומר אנושי, שאנו מכנים אותם בעלי החורבן. להיותם ממבקשי האמת, דהיינו להעמיד את העולם, על מדת שלי שלי ושלך שלך, שטבעי הוא, שאותם האנשים עומדים על דעתם בתוקף, עד להעמיד בסכנה את חייהם וחיי הצבור כולו.

והיא הנותנת להם תמיד את הכח, להתגבר על אותו חומר האנושי, בעלי הבנין, שהם ממבקשי החסד והצדקה, המוכנים לותר משלהם לטובת האחרים, כדי להציל את בנין העולם, שהמה הפחדנים מוגי הלב. באופן: שביקוש האמת וחורבן העולם, היינו הך. וביקוש החסד ובנין העולם, היינו הך. ולכן אין לקוות כלל מבעלי החורבן, שיבנה השלום על ידם.

וכן השלום המקווה, הוא מחוסר ערך לגמרי גם מצד הנשוא, כלומר, מצד התנאים של השלום עצמם, כי עדיין לא נבראו אותם התנאים המאושרים לחיי היחיד ולחיי הצבור, ע"פ על פי אמת המדה של מדת האמת, שעושי השלום הללו חפצים בה. והכרח הוא, שנמצאים וימצאו תמיד מיעוט חשוב בהחברה, בלתי מרוצים מהתנאים האלו, כמו שהוכחנו לעיל את חולשת האמת, אשר המה היו תמיד חומר מוכן, לבעלי הקטטה החדשים ולעושי השלום החדשים, שיתגלגלו כן לאין קץ.

The Entire World is One Community and One Society

It should not astonish you that I associate [lit. am putting together] the peace and wellbeing of a single community with the peace and wellbeing of the whole world because, in reality, we have reached such a level that the whole world is considered as only one community and one society. That is to say, since every individual in society derives his vitality and [the fulfillment of his] every need from the people of the entire world, he is thereby obliged to serve the entire world and to care for it.

We have demonstrated earlier, the total subservience of the individual to his community as a small cog that is subservient to a machine. This is because the individual derives all his life and all his happiness from the community, and therefore, the good of the community and his own individual good are one and the same, and vice versa. Therefore, to the same extent that a person is subservient to himself, he must become subservient to the community, as we have explained at length earlier.

Moreover, we should understand that the level of the community can be evaluated according to the extent to which the individual is provided for by that community. Because, for example, in ancient historical periods, the extent of subservience was only to one's family; that is to say, the individual did not need help from anyone except members of his own family, in which case he did not need to be subservient to anyone except members of his own family.

In later periods, families united to form towns and counties, and the individual became subservient to his town. And [even] later, when towns and counties became countries, the individual was helped with his well-being and happiness by all the members of the country, and thus he became subservient to the whole country.

כל העולם צבור אחד וחברה אחת

ולא יהיה זאת לתמיהא, מה שאני מערבב יחד את שלומו של צבור אחד, עם שלום העולם כולו, כי באמת כבר באנו לידי מדרגה כזו, שכל העולם נחשבים רק לצבור אחד ולחברה אחת. כלומר, שכל יחיד שבעולם, מתוך שיונק את לשד חייו והספקתו מכל בני העולם כולו, נעשה בזה משועבד, לשרת ולדאוג לטובת העולם כולו.

כי הוכחנו לעיל את השעבוד המוחלט של היחיד להצבור שלו, כדוגמת גלגל קטן בהמכונה, שהוא מטעם שנוטל כל חייו וכל אושרו מהצבור ההוא, וע"כ ועל כן , טובת הצבור וטובתו הפרטי היינו הך, וכן להיפך. ולפיכך, באותו השיעור שהאדם משועבד לעצמו, הנה בהכרח שנעשה משועבד להצבור, כמו שהארכנו בדברים לעיל.

ויש להבין עם זה, אשר שיעור הצבור ההוא שאמרנו, נבחן לפי מרחק יניקת היחיד מהם, כי למשל בתקופות ההסטורית הקדמוניות, היה מרחק הזה משוער רק במשפחה אחת, כלומר, שהיחיד לא נצרך לסיוע של מי שהוא רק מבני משפחתו לבדו, אשר אז ודאי, לא היה מוכרח להשתעבד [אלא] רק לבני המשפחה של עצמו.

ובתקופות מאוחרות נצטרפו המשפחות לעירות ולגלילות, ונעשה היחיד משועבד לעירו, ואחר כך כשנצטרפו העיירות והגלילות למדינות, והיה היחיד מסתייע באושר חייו מכל בני המדינה, הנה נעשה עם זה משועבד לכל המדינה.

This is why, in our generation, when every individual's happiness is affected [lit. being helped] by all the countries of the world, it must follow that this will be the extent to which the individual is subservient to the whole world—like the cog in a machine. And therefore, the possibility of peacefully creating good and happy procedures [order, government and justice] in one country, while neglecting to do so in all the countries of the world, is inconceivable. And vice versa, because in our day and age, our countries are already tied to [and dependent upon] each other as far as fulfilling their [citizens] life's needs is concerned, this is similar to ancient times, when individuals in families were dependent upon each other.

Therefore, nowadays we should not deal with and speak about orderly and just procedures for securing the peace of [only] one country or one nation, but should care only about the peace of the whole world because the welfare or calamity of every individual in the world is dependent on the extent of the welfare of individuals all over the world, and is measured according to it.

And even though these things have been known and actually concretely experienced to some degree, still the world has not properly and fully assimilated the concept, and this is because of the natural way a process develops, with action preceding understanding. This is why actions alone will teach humanity and push it forward.

ועל כן בדורינו זה, כשכל יחיד מסתייע באושר החיים שלו, מכל מדינות העולם, הנה הכרח הוא, שהיחיד נעשה בשיעור הזה משועבד לכל העולם כולו, כמו הגלגל בתוך המכונה. ולפיכך, אין להעלות על הדעת את האפשרות, לעשות סדרים טובים ומאושרים בדרכי שלום במדינה אחת, בשעה שלא יהיה כן בכל מדינות העולם, וכן להיפך, כי בתקופתינו אנחנו כבר מקושרים המדינות זו בזו בהספקת משאלות החיים, כמו היחידים במשפחתם בתקופות הקדמוניות.

ולפיכך אין לדבר ולעסוק עוד היום, מסדרים צודקים ומובטחים לשלום של מדינה אחת או אומה אחת, אלא רק משלום העולם כולו, כי טובתו ורעתו של כל יחיד ויחיד שבעולם, תלוי ומדוד במדת טובת היחידים שבכל העולם כולו.

ואף על פי, שדבר הזה כבר ידוע ומורגש למדי למעשה, עם כל זה עדיין העולם לא תפסו את זאת להלכה כראוי, והוא, להיות כן בטבע המהלכים של התפתחות, אשר המעשה מקדמת את עצמה להבנת הענינים, ורק המעשים יוכיחו וידחפו את האנושיות קדמה.

The Qualities of Mercy, Truth, Righteousness, and Peace Fight One Another

On top of all the above-mentioned practical difficulties that impede us—the helpless ones—on our path, we also have to deal with great confusion and inner conflict with regard to the psychological tendencies within us, meaning that those very qualities we have mentioned reside in each one of us, specifically and in conflict between one person to the other.

Specifically, this is because the four qualities that we have mentioned—Mercy and Truth and Righteousness and Peace, which are divided among the natures of human beings, whether through evolution or through education—these qualities themselves contradict each other.

Let us, for example, examine the quality of Mercy as an abstract. We find that the power of its dominion puts it in opposition to the other qualities. That is, when Mercy rules, there is no longer any place for the appearance of the rest of the qualities in our world because the quality of Mercy is understood and defined as a person saying, "Mine is Yours and Yours is Yours," as our sages said in the *Mishnah* (*Avot* 5).

And if the whole world would behave according to this quality [of Mercy], then all the high regard and great respect with which the world holds the qualities of Truth and Judgment would be cancelled and gone because when each of us is willing, of his own accord, to give everything he has to others and not to take back anything that belongs to the other, then any interest and reason to lie to one's peers is cancelled and gone. Nor is there any longer a need to speak about Truth because Truth and Falsehood are relative to each other, and if there was no Falsehood in this world, we would not have the concept of Truth in the world either.

מידות החסד, האמת, הצדק והשלום נלחמות זו בזו

והמעט לנו את הקושיים המעשיים הממשיים האמורים, המפריעים על דרכינו חדלי האונים, הנה נוסף לנו עוד ערבוביא ומלחמה גדולה, מבחינת הנטיות הפסיכולוגיות שבנו, כלומר מסבת המדות בעצמם השוררים בכל אחד מאתנו, באופן מיוחד, ובסתירה מאיש לרעהו.

והוא, להיות כי ארבע מדות הנזכרים חסד ואמת וצדק ושלום, שנתחלקו בטבעי בני אדם, אם מתוך ההתפתחות, ואם מתוך החינוך, הנה המדות הללו בעצמם סותרות המה זו לזו.

וכשנקח למשל את מדת החסד בצורה מופשטה, אנו מוצאים את כח ממשלתה, שסותרת את כל המדות האחרות, כלומר, שעל פי חוקי ממשלת החסד, אין שום מקום עוד, להופעת יתר המדות בעולמנו: כי מדת החסד מתפרשת ומוגדרת, בהאומר "שלי שלך ושלך שלך" כדברי חז"ל במשנה (אבות, פרק ה').

ואם היו בני העולם כולו מתנהגים במדתה זו, הרי בטלה והלכה לה כל התפארת והיקר שבמדת האמת, והדין, כי בשעה, שכל אחד מאתנו מוכן מטבעו ליתן את כל אשר לו לזולתו, ולא לקחת כלום מאשר לזולתו, הנה כבר בטל והלך לו כל ענין וכל גורם לשקר בעמיתו, ואין מקום לדבר אז ממדת האמת כל עיקר: כי האמת והשקר המה יחסיים זה לזה, ואם לא היה השקר בעולם, הנה אז לא היה לנו שום מושג של אמת בעולם.

Needless to say [in regards to] the other qualities [that is, Mercy, Righteousness, and Peace], they only emerged as a result of the weakness of Truth so that they might strengthen it, as explained earlier. And with regard to Truth, which is defined by the saying "Mine is Mine and Yours is Yours," it [Truth] is in opposition to the quality of Mercy and cannot stand it [Mercy] at all. This is because from the vantage point of Truth, it is completely unfair that one should work and toil for the sake of the other. Not only does one thereby make his friend fail, getting him accustomed to taking advantage of others, but Truth also teaches that each person must store some possessions for a rainy day so that he would not have to be a burden and live off the effort of others.

And on top of that, everyone has relatives who are heirs to his possessions. According to Truth, these relatives have higher priority than others, for that is what nature compels. Therefore, whoever gives all of his possessions away to others is, in fact, deceiving his relatives and heirs, in that he does not leave them anything to inherit.

In a similar fashion, Peace is in opposition to Righteousness because in order to create Peace in society, present conditions must remain as they are to guarantee that the energetic and clever become rich, while the neglectful and naïve remain poor. It means that a more dynamic individual ends up taking his own share as well as the share of his neglectful peers. And he lives a life of great luxury, so much so that nothing remains for the neglectful and the naïve, even to the point of their not being able to cover their most basic needs. Therefore, they remain naked with no possessions whatsoever but with many debt collectors.

It is obviously unjust to mete out such extreme punishment to the neglectful and naïve, who are innocent, for is it really a sin and a crime on their part that Providence has not bestowed upon those miserable [people] energy and cleverness? Should we punish them for this with such extreme suffering, which is even more difficult than

ואין צורך לומר שאר המדות, שהמה נצמחו ובאו רק מחולשת האמת כדי לחזק אותו, כנ"ל והאמת, המוגדר בהאומר "שלי שלי ושלך שלך" סותר למדת החסד, ואינו סובל אותו לגמרי, כי אין זה הגון כלל מבחינת האמת, לעמול ולהתיגע בשביל זולתו, כי מלבד שמכשיל את חברו ומרגילו עם זה לנצל את זולתו, הנה האמת נותן, שכל אדם מחויב לאצור לו רכוש לשעת הדחק, שלא יצטרך ליפול למעמסה על יגיעת זולתו.

ומלבד כל אלה, אין לך אדם שאין לו קרובים ויורש רכושו, שעל פי האמת הם מוקדמים לאחרים, כי כן הטבע מחייב, שהנותן כל רכושו לאחרים נמצא משקר בקרוביו ויורשיו, שאינו משאיר להם כלום שירשו אותו.

וכן השלום סותר לצדק, כי כדי לעשות שלום בהצבור, מוכרחים להיות התנאים כמות שהם קיימים, המבטיחים לפי תוכנם להזריזים והפקחים להיות עשירים, ואת המתרשלים והתמימים להיות עניים, באופן שכל בעל מרץ ביותר, נוטל חלקו וחלק חבריו המתרשלים. והוא חי בחיים טובים ביותר, עד שלא נשאר עוד להמתרשלים והתמימים, אפילו כדי חיותם ההכרחית, ונשארים ע"כ על כן בעירום ובחוסר כל ובנושים מרובים.

וזה ודאי בלתי צודק, להעניש את המתרשלים והתמימים במדה מרובה כל כך, על אשר לא חמס בכפיהם, ומה חטאם ומה פשעם של האומללים האלו, אם ההשגחה לא העניקה להם את הזריזות והפקחות, שמסבה זו נעניש אותם, ביסורים כאלו הקשים ממות? הרי שאין צדק כלל בתנאים של השלום, והשלום סותר לצדק.

death? This means that there is no Righteousness whatsoever in the conditions set by Peace. So Peace is in opposition to Righteousness. Likewise, Righteousness is in opposition to Peace, because if we arrange the allocation of wealth according to Righteousness, that is to say, give those who are neglectful and naïve an important portion that is relative to the energetic and the clever, surely those people of power and initiative will not rest or have peace until they topple such an administration that enslaves the great and energetic members and takes advantage of them for the sake of those weaklings. And therefore, there is no hope for public Peace. Thus, Righteousness is in opposition to Peace.

Thus you see how these qualities within us lock horns and clash with each other, not only between one faction of society and another, but within each individual as well. For these four qualities take hold of him or her, either all at once or one after the other, and wage war within him to the point that there is no way one could sort them out with the help of common sense and arrange them and bring them into one absolute agreement. On the contrary, each obstructs the other.

וכן הצדק סותר לשלום, כי אם נסדר את חלוקת הרכוש, על פי הצדק, דהיינו ליתן להמתרשלים והתמימים חלק חשוב בערך עם הזריזים ובעלי המרץ, הרי בעלי הכח והיזמה הללו, ודאי לא ינוחו ולא ישקיטו, עד להפיל את כל הנהלה ממין הזה, המשעבדת את הגדולים בעלי המרץ, ומנצלים אותם בשביל הנמושות הללו. ואין ע"כ על כן שום תקוה לשלום הצבור. הרי שהצדק סותר לשלום.

והנך רואה, איך המדות שבנו מנגחות ונלחמות זו בזו, ולא לבד בין כתות לכתות, אלא בכל אדם יחיד ג"כ גם כן, נמצאים הד' המדות הללו שולטים בו בבת אחת או בזה אחר זה, ונלחמות בקרבו עד שאין מקום להשכל הישר לסדר אותם ולהביאם, לידי הסכמה מוחלטת אחת, אלא שכל אחת מפריע על דרכה של חברתה.

The Root of All the Contradictions in the World

The truth is that the root of all this great confusion that prevails in us is none other than the Unique Individuality that we mentioned earlier, which is present in every one of us, to a lesser or greater degree. We have explained its beautiful and exalted and very grand purpose, inasmuch as this quality is extended to us directly from the Creator, who is the One and the Only One in the universe and the Root of all creatures. However, because it [the Unique Individuality] evolved into our narrow egoism, its action has become that of destruction and devastation. So much so, that it has become the source of all the destruction that was inflicted and will be inflicted in this world.

And you should know that not one human being in the world is free of [this Unique Individuality]. All the disagreements are only in the ways of using it; whether for the desires of the heart, or for governance, or for honor, these are the ways in which people differ from each other. But the equal aspect all the people of the world share is that every one of us is ready to take advantage of all the other people in the world for his own personal benefit, using every possible means at his disposal; not taking into account that in so doing, he is going to benefit himself on the basis of the destruction of the other.

The type of justification each person comes up with, according to his or her interests and point of view, does not matter whatsoever here. The Desire to Receive is the root of the mind; the mind is not the root of the desire. And frankly speaking, it can be said that the greater and more excellent a person is, to the same degree the quality of his Unique Individuality is greater and more prominent.

Now we will try to penetrate and understand the suitable conditions that would finally be accepted by humanity when the age of world peace appears in order to determine to what extent these conditions are suitable to bring a life of happiness to both the individual and society, and in order to examine the extent to which humanity as a whole is prepared to ultimately take on these sublime conditions.

שורש כל הסתירות שבעולם

והאמת הוא, ששורש כל הערבוביא הרבה הזאת השוררת בנו, אינו יותר, רק ממדת היחידיות הנזכר לעיל, המצויה בכל אחד ואחד מאתנו אם פחות ואם יותר, והגם שבארנו בה טעם יפה וגבוה מאד נעלה, אשר מדה זאת נמשך לנו ישר מהבורא ית' יחידו של עולם, שהוא שורש כל הבריות, עם כל זה מתוך שנתישבה בבחינת העגואיזם הצר שלנו, נעשית פעולתה לפעולת הריסה וחורבן, עד שהיתה למקור לכל החורבנות שהיו ויהיו בעולם.

ויש לדעת, שאין לך אף אדם אחד בעולם, שיהיה בן חורין ממנה, וכל החילוקים המה, רק באופני ההשתמשות עמה, אם לתאות לב, אם לממשלה, אם לכבוד, שבהם מתחלקים הבריות זה מזה, אבל הצד השוה שבכל בריות העולם הוא, שכל אחד מאתנו עומד לנצל לכל הבריות שבעולם לתועלתו הפרטית, בכל האמצעים שברשותו, ומבלי לקחת בחשבון כלל שהולך להבנות על חורבנו של חבירו.

ולא חשוב כאן כלום ההוראת התר, שכל אחד ממציא לעצמו על פי כיון המתאים לו, כי הרצון הוא שורש לכל שכל, ואין השכל שורש להרצון. והאמת ניתן להאמר, אשר כל שהאדם גדול ביותר ומצויין ביותר, הרי באותו השיעור ממש, מדת היחודיות שבו גדול ומצויין ביותר.

עתה נחדור להבין בתוך התנאים הישרים שיתקבלו סוף סוף על האנושות לעת הופעת הזמן של שלום העולם: לדעת במה כחם של התנאים הללו יפה עד להביא את החיי אושר להיחיד ולהצבור ולדעת את ההכנה שישנה בכלל האנושיות עד כדי לעמוס על עצמם לבסוף התנאים הגבוהים האלו.

The Two Sides of the Coin of Unique Individuality

So let us return to the issue of the Unique Individuality in the heart of each person, which is ready to swallow up the world in its entirety for its own pleasure. We shall consider the previously mentioned question regarding the importance and glory of the root [of this Unique Individuality] as an extension directly from the One and Only of the universe [the Creator] to humans, who are His branches, as mentioned earlier. This question is valid and demands an answer: How is it that it [Unique Individuality] manifests within us in such a distorted fashion, becoming the root cause and progenitor of all the destroyers and ruin-mongers of the world? How could the source of all construction bring about, so directly, the source of all destruction? Such questions cannot be set aside without an answer.

Indeed, there are two sides to the coin of this Unique Individuality. If we examine it from the point of view of one side, the exalted side, which means from the aspect of its affinity with the One and Only of this universe [the Creator], it [the Unique Individuality] operates only through the mode of "sharing with others." After all, the Creator is there entirely for the sake of sharing. He does not have any trace of receiving in Him because He lacks nothing and does not need to receive anything from His creatures—His own created beings. Therefore, the Unique Individuality that is extended to us from Him must, of necessity, operate also in the form of "sharing with others" rather than "receiving for himself."

But looking at the other side of the same coin—from the lower, second aspect, that is, from the point of view of the way it [the Unique Individuality] functions within us in practice—we find that it behaves in a completely opposite manner [lit. direction] because it operates only in the form of "receiving for oneself," for example, as an ambition to be the single wealthiest person in the whole world, or the single most honored person in the whole world, etc. In the end, therefore, these two aspects form two extremes that are as distant from each other as possible, just as East is distant from West.

שני הצדדים שבהמטבע היחודיות

ונחזור לדבר היחידיות שבלב כל אדם העומדת לבלוע להנאתה את כל העולם ומלואה כי השאלה הנזכרת בדבר החשיבות ותפארת שורשה שהיא נמשכת ישר מיחידו של עולם לבני האדם שהם ענפיו כנזכר לעיל. הריהי עומדת ותובעת לעצמה תשובה איך יצוייר לה להגלות בתוכינו בצורה מקולקלת כזאת ולהעשות לאבי אבות כל מזיקי ומחריבי עולם ומהמקור של כל בנין יתמשך ישר ויצא, המקור של כל חורבן. ואי אפשר להניח שאלה כזאת, בלי פתרון.

אמנם יש שני צדדים, בהמטבע של היחודיות האמורה, כי אם נסתכל בה מצדה הא' העליונה דהיינו מצד השתוותה עם יחידו של עולם, הרי היא פועלת רק בצורות של "השפעה לזולתו", שהרי הבורא ית' כולו להשפיע הוא עומד, ואין בו מצורות של קבלה ולא כלום, כי לא חסר לו מאומה, ואינו צריך לקבל דבר מבריותיו שברא. ולכן, גם היחודיות שנמשך בנו ממנו ית', מחויבת שתפעיל גם כן רק בצורות של "השפעה לזולתו" , ולא כלום "לקבל לעצמו".

ומצד הב' של אותו המטבע, דהיינו אם נסתכל בה מצדה הב' התחתונה, דהיינו מבחינת צורת פעולתה המעשיית שפועלת בנו, נמצאת שפועלת בכיון הפוך לגמרי, כי פועלת רק בצורות של "קבלה לעצמו". כגון, להיות העשיר הגדול היחידי שבכל העולם, או המכובד הגדול היחידי שבכל העולם, וכדומה. באופן, שב' הצדדים האמורים, הם ב' קצוות רחוקים זה מזה בתכלית המרחק, כרחוק מזרח ממערב.

The Solution

Herein we find the answer to the question we asked earlier: How is it that the same Unique Individuality, which springs forth and reaches us from the One and Only of the universe, Who is the Source of all construction, serves in us as the source of all destruction? All this has happened to us because we are using this precious vessel [Unique Individuality] in an opposite manner [lit. direction], as we have explained. I am not claiming that the Unique Individuality within us absolutely never acts in the form of "sharing with others," reflecting side A, which we discussed earlier. We cannot deny that there are people among us in whom Unique Individuality operates in order to share with others, such as those who spend lavishly of their own wealth for the benefit of society with noticeable excellence, surpassing anyone else in the world, and also those who spend all their energy for the sake of society, etc.

But these two sides of the coin, which I have described, speak only about the two points in the evolution of Creation—[an evolution] that brings everything to its perfection. It [the evolution] starts from absence,[3] and slowly and gradually climbs up the ladder of evolution, from a lower level to a higher one, and from [that level] to a yet higher one, until it reaches the goal at the height of its climb,[4] which is its predetermined degree of perfection, where it rests, remaining in that state for eternity.

In this sequence of development, there are two points: the initial point, which is the lowest stage and is very close to the complete emptiness, which is the point described as the second side of the coin; and the zenith of evolution, where it will rest and remain for eternity, and which was earlier described as the first side of the coin.

3. Pure Desire to Receive, no sharing
4. Sharing with no agenda

הפתרון

ומצאנו בזה הפתרון למה ששאלנו, איך אפשר שאותו היחידיות הנובעת ומגעת אלינו מיחידו של עולם, שהוא המקור לכל בנין, תהיה משמשת בנו למקור לכל חורבן? כי זה הגיע לנו, מתוך שאנו משמשים עם כלי היקרה הזאת בכיון הפוך, כאמור. ואיני אומר, שהיחודיות שבנו לא יארע לה לעולם, שתפעול בנו בצורות "השפעה לזולתו" כמו צד הא' הנזכר, כי אי אפשר להכחיש, שנמצא בתוכנו אנשים, שהיחודיות פועל בהם גם בהשפעה לזולתם, כמו המפזרים רכושם לטובת הכלל, בהצטיינות ניכר, העולה על כל העולם, וכן המפזרים כל יגיעותם לטובת הכלל, וכדומה.

אלא אותם ב' הצדדים שבהמטבע, שתיארתי, מדברים רק מב' הנקודות, שבהתפתחות הבריאה, המביאה לכל דבר על שלמותו. שהיא מתחלת מההעדר, ומטפסת ועולה במדרגות ההתפתחות לאט לאט, ממדרגה הנמוכה למדרגה גבוה ממנה, ומשם ליותר גבוה, עד הגיעה על תכלית גבהה, דהיינו במדת השלימות הקצובה לה מראש, אשר שמה כבר תנוח ונשארת קיימת כן לנצח.

אשר יש בסדר התפתחות הזה ב' נקודות, דהיינו: נקודת ההתחלה, שהיא שלובה (שלב) התחתונה הקרובה להעדר הגמור, שהיא המתוארת לצד הב' של המטבע. ונקודת תכלית הגובה, ששמה תנוח ותשאר קימת לנצחיות, היא המתוארת בצד הא' של המטבע.

Surely, this period that we find ourselves in, is already quite developed, having passed through many levels [in the evolutionary process]. It has ascended from the lowest stage, which is the above-mentioned side B, and has considerably approached side A. This is why there are those among us who use the Unique Individuality within them in the "sharing with others" mode. But because we are still halfway through the process of evolution, these people are still rare. And when we finally reach the zenith, the topmost final level, then we will all use our Unique Individuality solely in the "sharing with others" mode. It will not occur to anyone that could use it in the "receiving for oneself" mode, meaning like side B of the coin.

אמנם תקופה זו, שאנחנו נמצאים בה, כבר התפתחה במדה מרובה, ועלתה כבר מדרגות רבות, דהיינו במדה, שהתרוממה למעלה משלובה (שלב) התחתונה, שהיא צד הב' הנזכר, והתקרבה במדה ניכרת אל צד הא' ועל כן כבר נמצאים בנו אנשים המשמשים עם היחודיות שבהם בצורות של "השפעה לזולתו" אלא שעדיין מועטים המה להיותינו נמצאים עוד באמצע הדרך של ההתפתחות. וכשנגיע לנקודת הגובה סוף כל המדרגות אז כולנו נשמש בהיחודיות שלנו רק בצורות של השפעה לזולתו ולא יארע פעם לשום אדם שישמש עמה בצורות של "קבלה לעצמו": דהיינו לגמרי, כצד הא' של המטבע.

The Lifestyle of the Final Generation[5]

Based on these thoughts, we now have the possibility of looking into the lifestyle of the final generation, which is the time when world peace will prevail. In other words, this is the time when humanity as a whole will reach the summit of evolution, or side A of the coin. This will be the time when Unique Individuality will be used only in the "sharing with others" mode and not at all in the "receiving for oneself" mode. And it would be worth our while to copy [describe] their way of life, both the life of the individual and the life of the society, in a way that will teach us valuable lessons, and in order for it to be incorporated even in the flooding torrents of our lives. Maybe it would be possible and worthwhile to make an experiment and adopt this mode of life even in our present generation.

To begin with, it would be appropriate to start with the most exalted thing which, most probably, is the foundation on which the whole structure of that society is based and by which it is supported. They [members of that society] have invested a great and boundless effort to create for themselves a classical literary treasure chest of books of wisdom, edited with great dialectical skill. The purpose [of these books] is to cultivate a unique worldview with regard to "sharing with others" and to bring about the manifestation of such a view. [These books] capture the hearts of so many that all the people, from the least to the greatest, are completely immersed in them with great delight. Their houses of justice are completely busy with giving out "titles of distinction" to people, who actually demonstrate an achievement of a certain level of "sharing with others." There is no one who does not carry on his sleeve such a title of distinction of one level or another. Public opinion holds these title bearers in high regard and honor.

5. The end of the correction process

תנאי החיים של הדור האחרון

ועל פי דברים הללו מצאנו לנו הזדמנות להסתכל בתנאי החיים של דור האחרון, כלומר שבעת הופעת הזמן של שלום העולם דהיינו בזמן שהאנושיות כולה תגיע לנקודת הגובה לצד הא' של המטבע ויהיו משמשים עם היחידיות שבהם רק בצורות של "השפעה לזולתו" ולא כלל בצורות של "קבלה לטובת עצמו". וכדאי להעתיק [לתאר] כאן את צורות החיים שלהם מחיי היחיד לחיי החברה במדה שתשמש אלינו לקח למופת ולהתיישב תחת שטף גלי החיים שלנו. אולי כדאי ואפשר גם בדורנו זה לעשות איזה נסיון להתלבש בצורות החיים שלהם.

ומתחילה ראוי להקדים את הדבר הנכבד ביותר שכפי הנראה הוא היסוד שכל בנין החברה ההיא נבנה ונשען עליו והוא, כי ביגיעה גדולה למעלה מכל גבול המציאו לעצמם יצירה ספרותית קלאסית מספרי חכמה הערוכים באמנות דיאלקטית רבה המסגלים ומביאים לידי גילוי של תפיסת עולם מיוחדת מבחינת "השפעה לזולתו" והמה צודים כ"כ) כל כך(לבבות עד שכל העם מגדלם עד קטנם עסוקים בהם ראשם ורובם בהנאה עמוקה. הבתי משפט שלהם מלאים עבודה מחלוקת "תוארי כבוד" להעם המציינים את מדרגת השגה המעשיית שזכו בהשפעה לזולתו, ואין אדם שלא יהיה מזוין בתואר כבוד מאיזה מדרגה על שרוולו ודעת הקהל מחשיב ומכבד מאד את משיגי התוארי כבוד ממדרגות החשובים.

Great competition has evolved among the people around the sphere of activity of "sharing with others," to the point that they sometimes bring themselves into great dangers. A person who has failed with regard to some aspect [of his work] and has acted for his own benefit [instead of sharing with others] may experience how his social standing disappears in the stream of social life just like clouds disappear in the wind because of the deep aversion that all levels of society [now] feel towards him.

If we do not take into consideration the loss of titles of distinction due to guilt, the laws of justice of their [the final generation's] courts do not include any form of punishment, and furthermore, every defendant comes out of the house of justice with some profit. For example, if the indictment concerns negligence at work, the verdict is usually to add to the rations of his sustenance so that he would get healthier or to reduce the hours of his work. Only rarely does it happen that the defendant is sent to an institution of special education in order to improve his consciousness.

Each person fulfills his role in the service of the public with utter perfection and without any supervision because the public opinion puts pressure on each one, both openly and in hidden ways, to the point that the person feels, in his bones, the severity of the crime of even a slight betrayal of the public trust in the [same] way that our person feels the crime of murdering another.

התחרות גדולה התפתחה בהעם על שדה פעולה "מהשפעה לזולתו" עד שמביאים עצמם לפעמים מחמת זה גם בסכנות עצומות. אדם שנכשל באיזה עובדה לתועלתו הפרטית הרי כל עמידתו החברתית התנדפה והלכה לה באויר החיים של החברה כעננים על פני רוח מחמת האנטיפטיא העמוקה מכל שדרות העם אליו.

אם לא להתחשב עם אבידת תוארי הכבוד מחמת אשמה לא נמצא בחוקי המשפט שלהם שום צורה של עונש ולא עוד אלא למעשה יוצא כל נאשם מבית המשפט עם רווח למשל עם האשמה היא בהתרשלות בעבודה יוצא הפסק דין על פי רוב או להוסיף לו על סדרי מזונותיו שיבריא יותר או להפחית לו את מספר שעות עבודתו ולעתים רחוקים מאד יארע גם כן ששולחים את הנאשם לבית חינוך מיוחד לאלו כדי להטיב הפסיכולוגיא שלו.

כל אחד מהם ממלא את תפקידו בשרות הצבור בתכלית השלימות בלי שום השגחה כי דעת הקהל לוחץ על כל אדם כבגלוי כבסתר עד שהאדם מרגיש בעצמותיו את חומר העון ממשהו אונאת הצבור במדה שהאדם שלנו מרגיש את העון של רציחת נפש.

Mandatory Work and Voluntary Work

The difference in status in society between those who are negligent [or slow] and those who are energetic is obvious and apparent: The status of those who are negligent [or slow] is very low because the Supreme Providence has taken all honor away from them. Each group—that is, a certain number of people with sufficient means to cover all their needs and make them independent of others—has its own administration with an allotment of a certain number of work hours according to the conditions of their location. This is done in a way that there will be enough to provide for all their needs. The allotment [of work hours] is filled by the members through mandatory work hours and voluntary work hours.

There are four kinds of mandatory work hours, and each person, in complete trustworthiness and on his own accord, must assign himself to [one form of these mandatory work hours], in accordance with his ability. The first kind [of mandatory work hours] relates to the weaklings in the community, who are committed to one hour of work per day. The second kind relates to the healthy who commit themselves to two hours of work. The third kind relates to the strong ones who will commit to four hours, and the fourth kind relates to the most energetic ones who are committed to eight hours a day. These are the mandatory work hours. In addition, there are members of all four kinds who undertake voluntary work hours out of their strong will to "share with others." The proceeds from voluntary work create a basis of wealth for the community, and this wealth is there to support communities in all countries who are lagging behind.

שעות חובה ושעות נדבה

ההפרש המעמדי שבהצבור בולט וניכר לעין בין המתרשלים ובין הזריזים כי מעמד המתרשלים ירוד מאד בהחברה כי ההשגחה העליונה מנעה אותם מכבוד. כל חברה, דהיינו מספר אנשים עם אמצעים המספיקים לכל צרכם שעושה אותם בלתי תלויים באחרים, יש לה הנהלה משלה עם תקציב של מספר שעות עבודה בהתאם לתנאי המקום שלהם באופן שיספיקו לכל משאלותיהם אשר תקציב הזה מתמלא על ידי החברים משעות חובה ומשעות נדבה.

השעות חובה באים מד׳ סוגים שכל אדם נאמן על עצמו להכנס להסוג שהוא בהתאם עם כחו: סוג הא׳ הם החלושי כח שבהחברה מתחייבים בשעה אחת ליום, סוג ב׳ הבריאים מהם מתחייבים בב׳ שעות, סוג ג׳ האמיצי כח בד׳ שעות, סוג ד׳ הזריזים ביותר מתחייבים בשמונה שעות ליום. אלו המה שעות חובה ומלבד זה נמצאים חברים מכל הד׳ סוגים שנותנים שעות נדבה מתוך רצונם החזק ״בהשפעה לזולתו״ שהיוציר משעות נדבה אלו בונה אוצר להחברה והאוצר הזה קיים לתמוך בחברות נחשלות בכל הארצות.

How to Adapt the Lifestyle of the Future Generation in Our Generation

I imagine now that there is not much need to go on for too long about the lifestyle of the future generation because even the things that I have already said will stimulate the interest of any intelligent person to contemplate and see how well-adapted and qualified [this lifestyle is] for this generation of ours. And I will also try to elaborate about this because I believe that there is a possibility to incorporate in the near future these ways of life even in the way that we ourselves live today; it depends only on understanding.

That is to say, to explain to the leaders of our generation…
And we have already spoken about it previously…
[Rav Ashlag wrote these two lines and then crossed them out]

First of all, everyone must understand well and explain to [people] in his or her vicinity that the peace of society, that is, the peace of the country and the peace of the world, are completely interdependent, because as long as the laws of society do not fulfill the wants of every individual in the country but leave some minority dissatisfied by the way society is governed, that minority shall scheme against the government and seeks to topple it.

And if they [the minority] are not powerful enough to fight face-to-face with the government from within, then it may try to overthrow [the government] indirectly. The easiest way to accomplish this is to incite one government against another and to get them [countries] to fight with one another because it is natural that in times of war, their [the dissatisfied] power will be augmented by the addition of many disgruntled people from within the country. In this way, they hope to gain a decisive majority and overthrow their country's government and erect a government that is most suitable for them. This makes it clear that the peace of an individual country is a direct cause of world peace.

איך להנהיג את סגנון חיי דור העתיד בדורנו זה

אשער לעצמו כעת שאין צורך להאריך ולתאר יותר מתנאי החיים של דור העתיד כי גם הדברים שהבאתי כבר נותנים ענין רב לכל בר דעת להתבונן בהם על כמה שהמה מסוגלים ומתאימים לדורינו זה וגם אני אנסה לשאת וליתן בהדבר כי לדעתי יש אפשרות לא רחוק ביותר להנהיג הסדרים הללו גם בסדרי החיים שלנו אלא רק בהבנה תלוי הדבר.

כלומר להסביר למנהיגי הדור
וכבר הבאנו לעיל
[הרב אשלג כתב שתי שורות אלה ומחק אותן]

ראשית כל צריך כל אחד להבין היטב ולהסביר את הסביבה שלו אשר שלום החברה דהיינו שלום המדינה ושלום העולם תלוים זה בזה לגמרי כי כל כמה שחוקי החברה אינם משביעים רצון לכל יחיד ויחיד שבהמדינה אלא שמשאירים מיעוט בלתי מרוצים מהנהלת החברה הרי המיעוט הזה חותר תחת הנהלה זו ומבקש להפילה.

ואם אין כחו מספיק להלחם עם הנהלת המדינה פנים בפנים הריהו צודה להפיל אותם בדרך עקיפין שדבר הקרוב להם ביותר הוא לשסות הממשלות זו בזו ולהביאם לידי מלחמה. כי טבעי הוא שבעת מלחמה נוסף עליהם הרבה בלתי מרוצים מבני המדינה ואז יש תקוה להם להשיג רוב מכריע ולהפיל הנהלת המדינה ולהקים הנהלה כזו הנוח להם ביותר. הרי ששלום הפרטי של המדינה הוא גורם ישר לשלום העולם.

World Peace and the Peace of the Country Are Interdependent

Moreover, if you take into account the section of the population of the country who are experts in war and for whom conflict is their hope for success—for example, war experts [military] and weapons industry, who form a very important minority in the country as far as the quality of society—and if you add to them the minority that is not content with the rules that govern the country, then you can see that at any given time, most of the people of the country are looking forward to wars and bloodshed. This is a very practical demonstration that world peace and the peace of a country are intertwined and interdependent.

And if this is the case, it necessarily follows that even those of the country's population who are satisfied with the present laws, meaning the energetic ones and the clever ones, are still very concerned about the safety of their lives because of the absence of peace in the world. And what sort of satisfaction might one find when he knows that most of the people in his country are scheming against his life? If everyone understood this, they would probably be happy to completely accept the above-mentioned lifestyle of the final generation because everyone will gladly give everything they possess to protect their life.

שלום העולם ושלום המדינה תלויים זה בזה

ולא עוד אלא אם תקח בחשבון את אותו החלק הנמצא תמיד בהמדינה אשר המלחמה היא אומנותם וכל תקות הצלחתם, כמו המלומדי מלחמה והעוסקים בהספקת צרכי זיון שמבחינת האיכות החברתי הם מיעוט חשוב מאד בהמדינה, ואם עוד תצרף עליהם את המיעוט שאינם מרוצים מחוקים הקיימים בהמדינה הרי לפניך בכל שעה ושעה רוב בנין גדול בהמדינה המשתוקקים למלחמות ושפיכת דמים. מבחינת המעשיית הרי ששלום העולם ושלום המדינה תלויים זה בזה.

ואם כן הוא, נמצא בהכרח, שאפילו אותו החלק שבהמדינה אשר מרוצים כעת מהחוקים הקיימים דהיינו הזריזים והפקחים עדיין עומד לפניהם דאגה רבה לבטחון חייהם מחמת חוסר השלום בעולם. ואיזה סיפוק נפשי מוצא אדם בשעה שיודע שרוב בני המדינה חותרין תחת חייו, ואם היו מבינים את זאת היו שמחים בודאי לקבל בהחלט את סדרי החיים הנזכרים של דור האחרון כי כל אשר לאדם יתן בעד נפשו.

People Produce More than They Receive

And when we look closely and grasp well, with our minds, the above-mentioned plan of the final generation, we will come to realize that the core of difficulty and heaviness is in transforming our nature from the Desire to Receive for Oneself to the Desire to Share with others. Seemingly, these two [desires] oppose each other, and at first sight, it may seem just like some general fantasy, something that is beyond human nature—at least as far as most of humanity are concerned. Indeed, when we look deeply into it, we will find that the contradiction between "receiving for oneself" and "sharing with others" is not only in the psychological aspect.

In reality, there is not a single person in the world who receives for himself, but rather, we all share with others without deriving any reward for our own benefit. This is because although the Receiving for oneself has been described as having different elements—from possessions and property to various luxuries that please the heart, the eye, the stomach [lit. palate], etc.—when in fact, all these are defined by one term: pleasure. It follows, that the entire essence of Receiving for Oneself that one desires for, is none other than his desire for pleasure.

And now imagine for yourself if we put all the different kinds of pleasure that we obtain during our 70 years to one side, and all the sorrow and troubles that we suffer during those 70 years to the other side, weighed them against each other, and presented them to a person just before he is born. Anyone with any intelligence would swear that no person would choose to be born of his own accord because there is not one person in this world whose troubles are not 77 times more than his pleasure throughout his life. And if this is the case, what does one get out of living in this world?

האדם יוצר יותר ממה שמקבל

והנה כאשר נסתכל ונתפוס בשכלינו היטב את התכנית הנזכר של דור האחרון הנה כל נקודת הקושי והכובד מונחת בהתהפכות הטבע שלנו מן הרצון לקבל לעצמו עד הרצון להשפיע לזולתו. כי לכאורה המה ב' דברים המכחישים זה את זה, ובהשקפה ראשונה מדומה זה רק לפאנטאזיע [פנטזיה] בעלמא ולדבר שלמעלה מהטבע האנושי ועל כל פנים ממרבית האנושיות. אמנם כאשר נעמיק בדבר נמצא אשר כל הסתירה מקבלה לעצמו להשפעה לזולתו איננה רק מבחינה פסיכולוגית בלבד.

כי למעשה אין לך אדם בעולם שיהיה מקבל לעצמו, אלא כולנו רק משפיעים לזולתינו בלי שום טובת הנאה כלל לתועלתו עצמו הפרטית. כי הקבלה עצמית אף על פי שמתוארת אצלינו במינים שונים מרכוש וקנינים ומחמדי הלב, העין, והחיך וכדומה הרי כל אלו מוגדרים רק בשם אחד של תענוג. באופן שכל עיקר הקבלה לעצמו שאדם מתאוה אין זה אחרת אלא שרוצה להתענג.

ועתה צא ודמה לך אם נקבץ כל שיעורי התענוג שמשיג האדם במשך שבעים שנותיו לצד אחד ונקבץ את כל הצער והיסורים שסובל במשך שבעים שנותיו לצד השני בב' מערכות לעיני אותו האדם בטרם שנולד, הרי כל בעל שכל יוכל להשבע ששום בן אדם לא היה מסכים מדעתו להולד. כי אין לך אדם בעולמנו היום שאין היסורין עולים פי שבעים ושבעה על התענוג שלו שבמשך ימי חייו. ואם כן הוא הדבר, איזה קבלה לעצמו משיג האדם בעולמו.

Make a simple mathematical calculation: Suppose a person has 20 percent pleasure and 80 percent trouble in his life. If you subtract 20 from 80, you see that 60 percent of the suffering is without any reward. So from here, you can measure the actual [amount of] receiving, which is actually available for that person. Indeed, those 60 percent of suffering that remained without any [positive] return are considered a deficit only to that one person, still, if we do a general worldly calculation, here for the first time [we realize that] a person produces more than he receives for his own existence and enjoyment.

ועשה לך חשבון מתימתי פשוט נניח שיש להאדם בימי חייו עשרים אחוזים תענוג ושמונים אחוזים יסורין וקח ונכה את העשרים אחוזים של תענוג מהשמונים של יסורין ישאר בידך ששים אחוזים יסורים בלי שום תמורה, ואמוד מעתה את הקבלה עצמית האפשרית להאדם למעשה. אמנם אין הששים אחוזים יסורין הללו שנשארו בלי תמורה נחשבים לדעפיציט גרעון אלא רק לאותו האדם עצמו, אמנם אם תעשה חשבון עולמי כללי הנה סוף סוף האדם יוצר יותר ממה שמקבל לקיומו ולהנאתו.

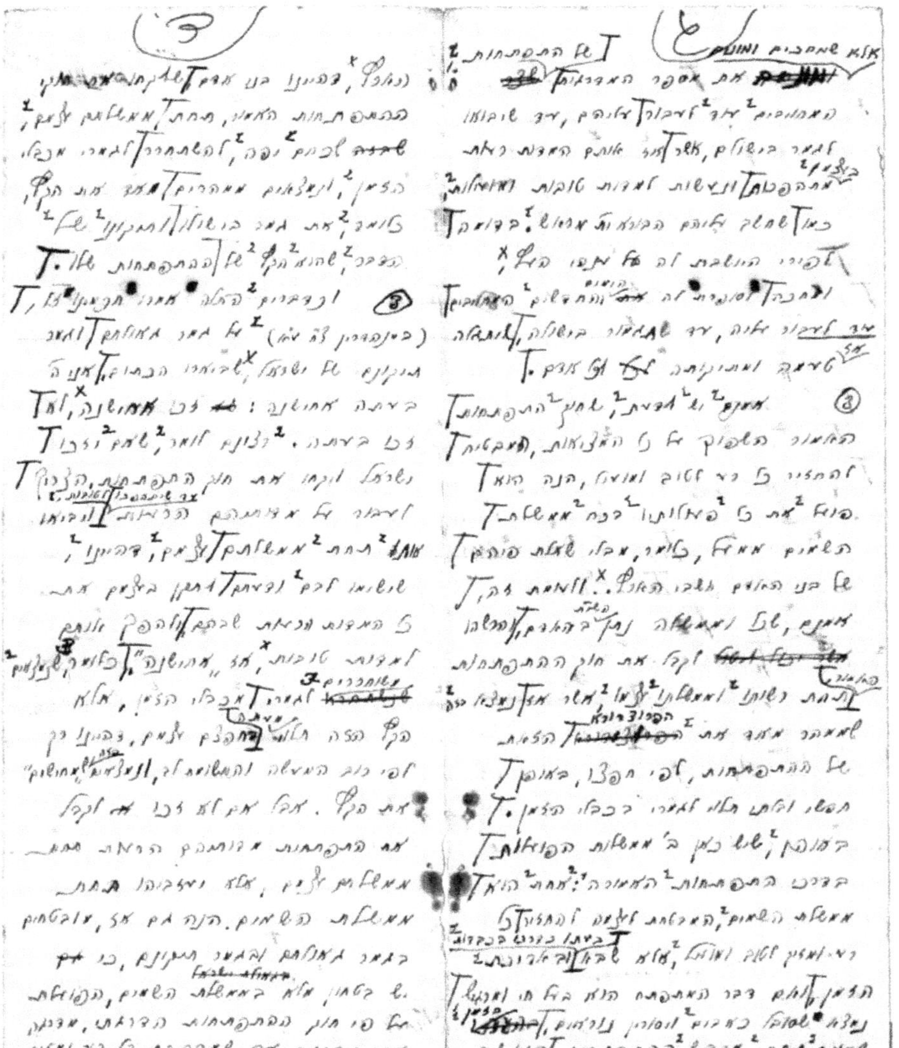

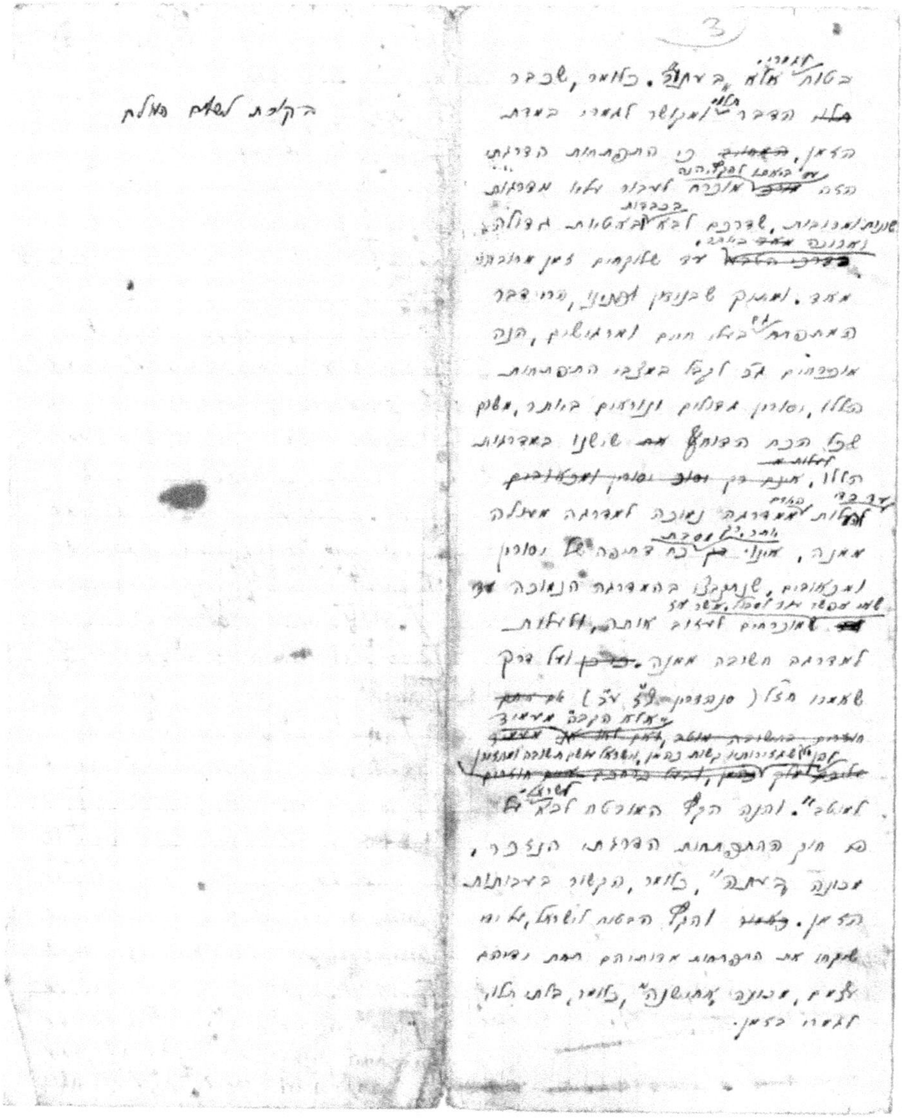

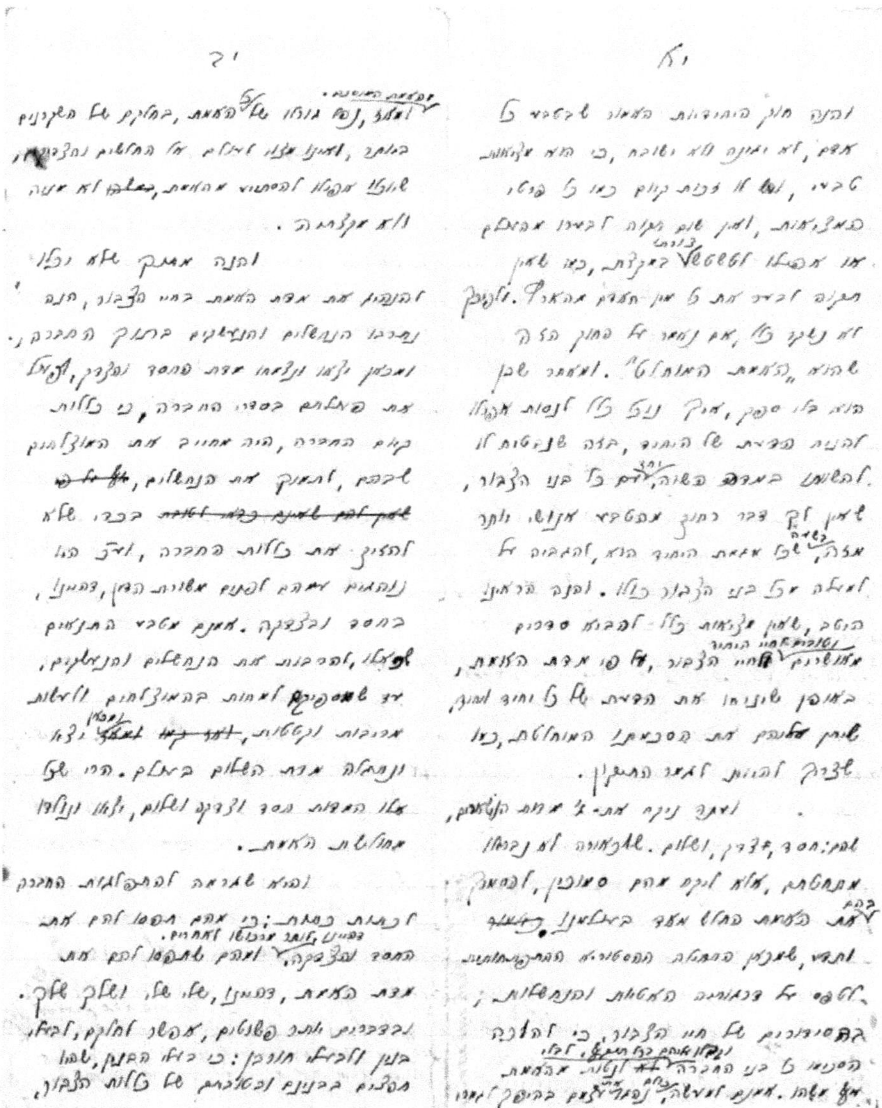

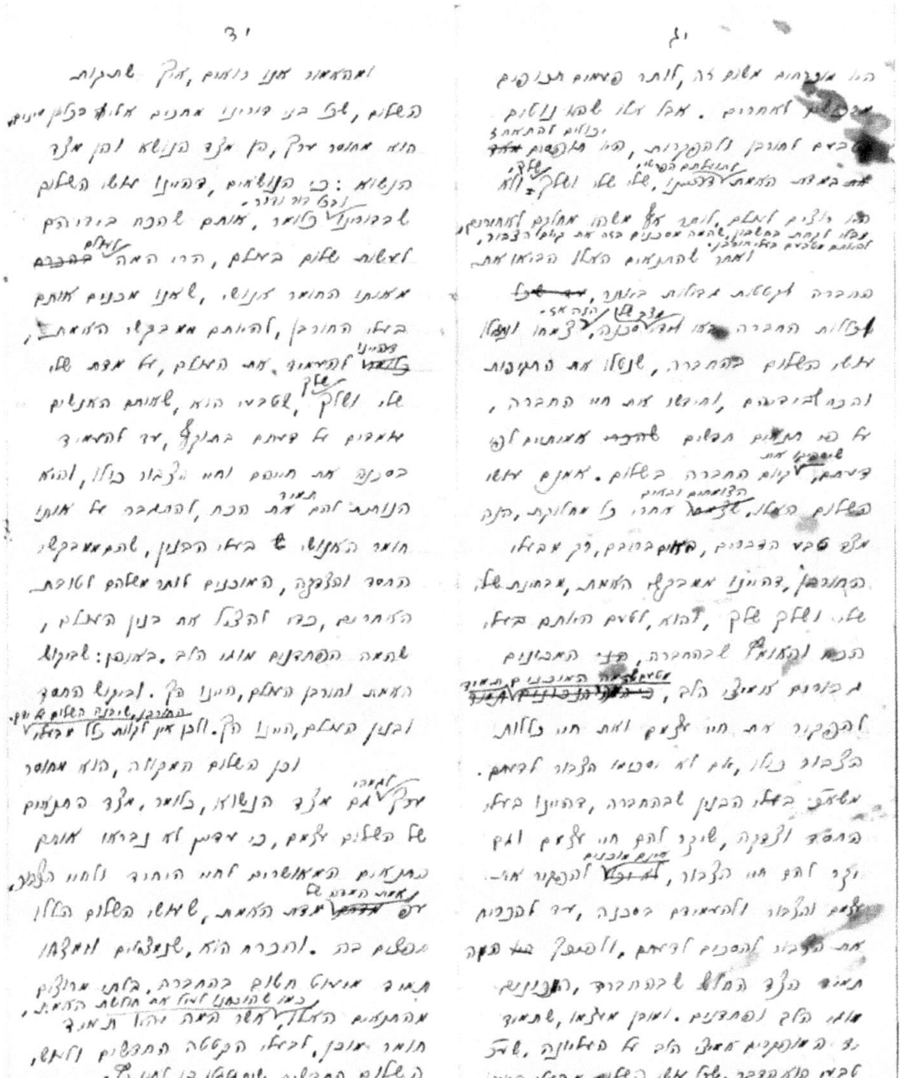

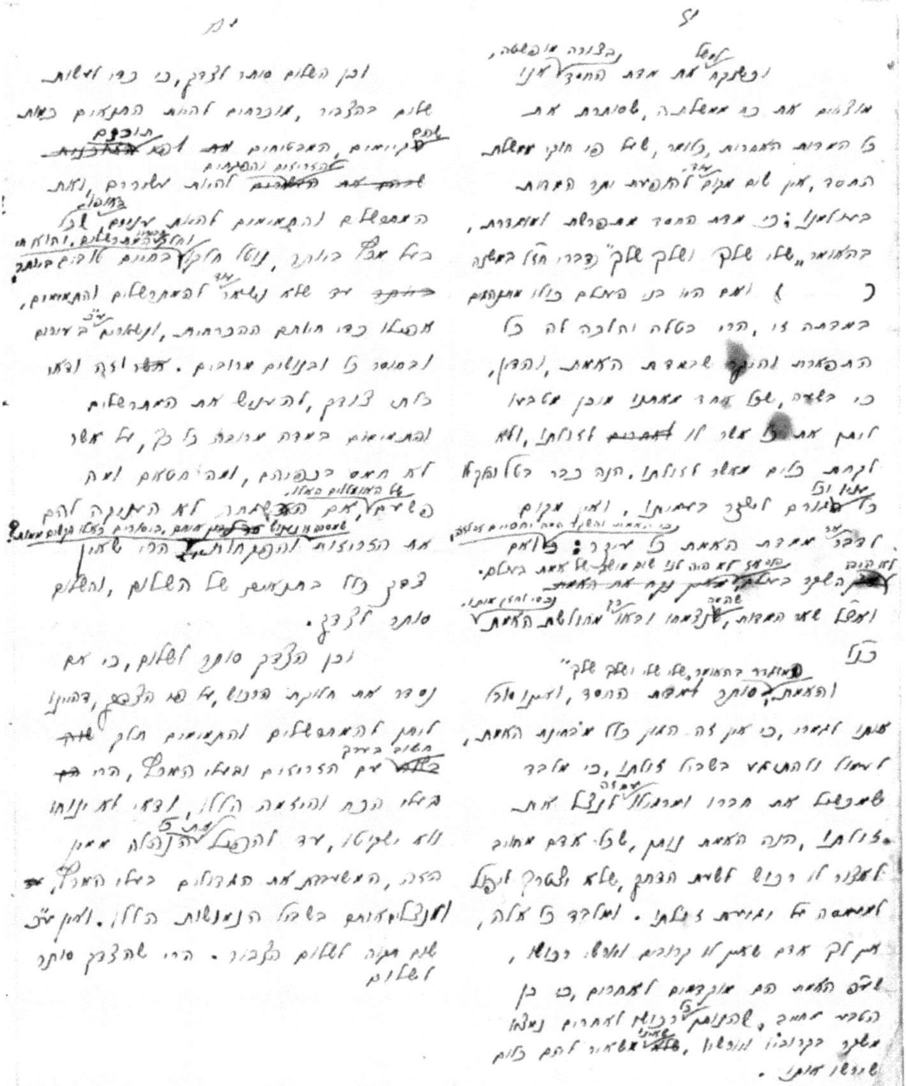

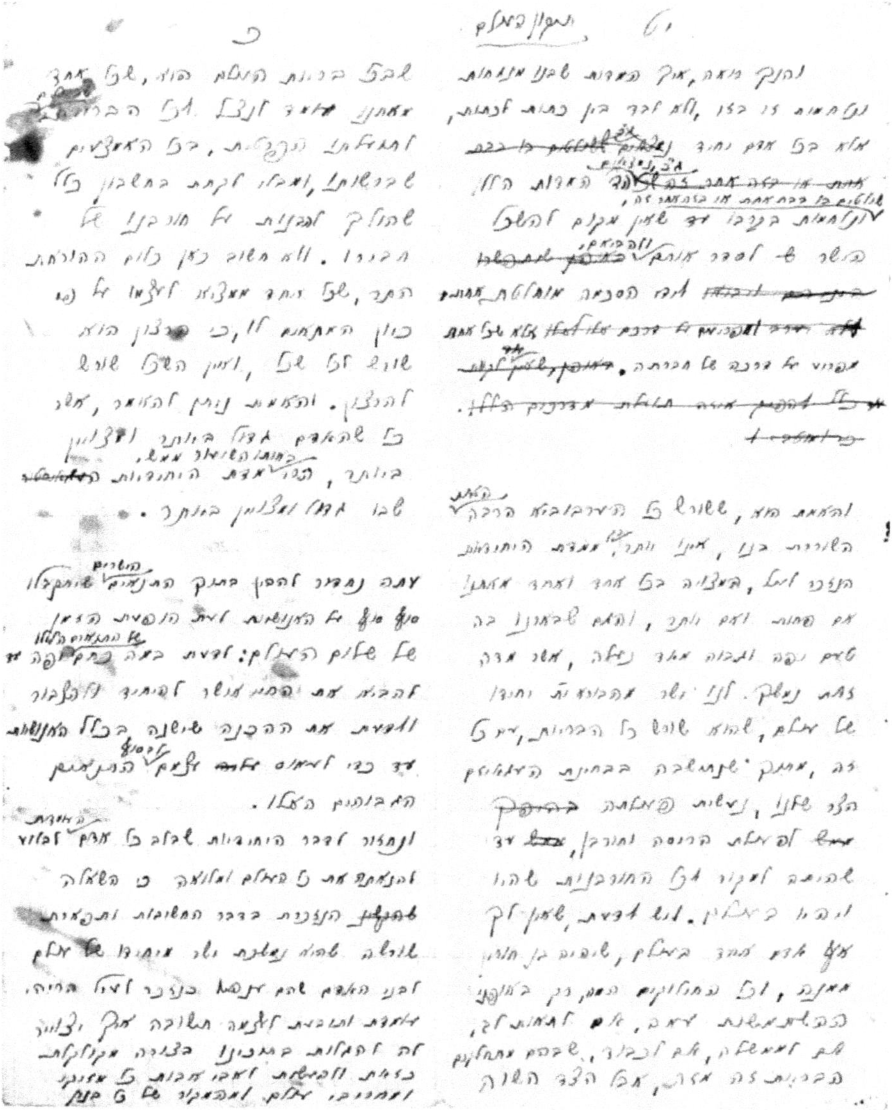

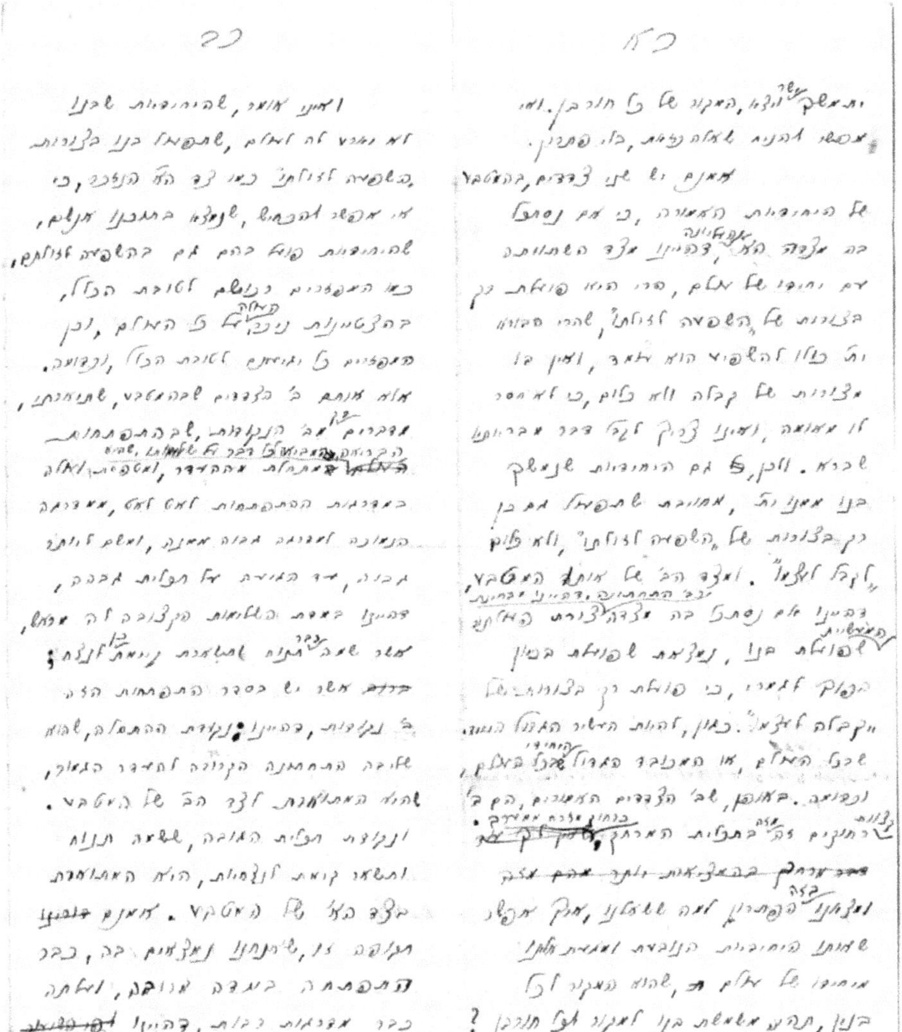

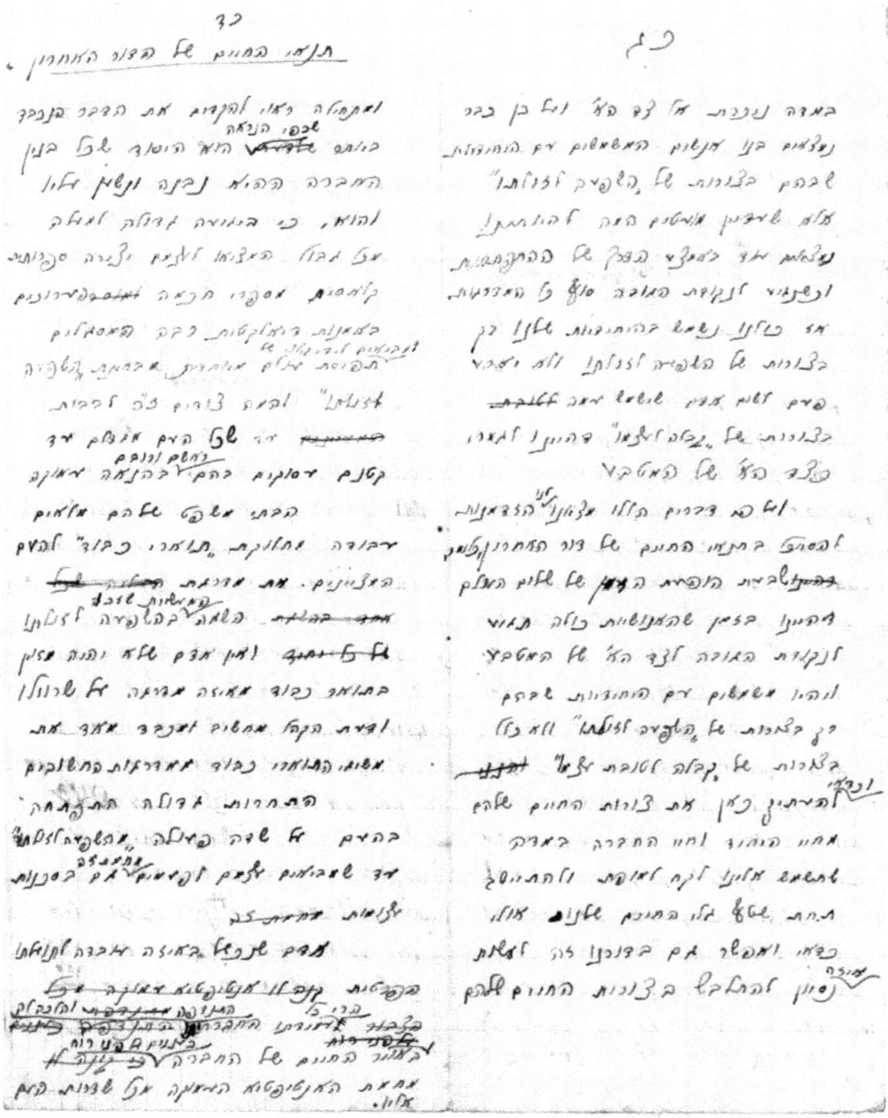

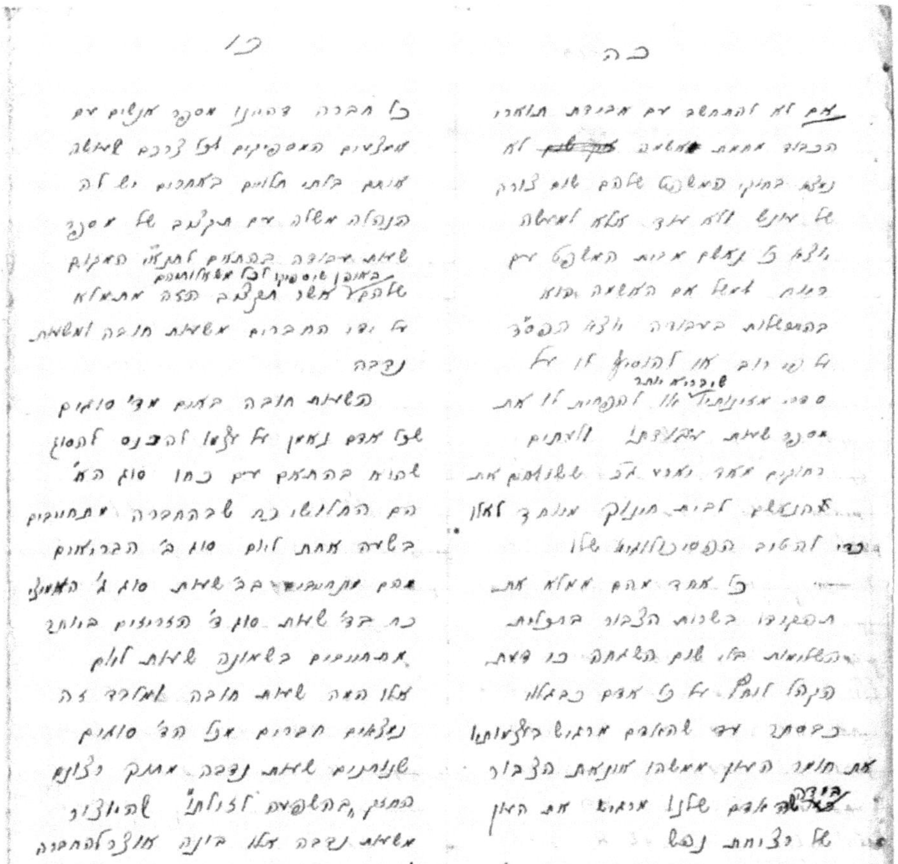

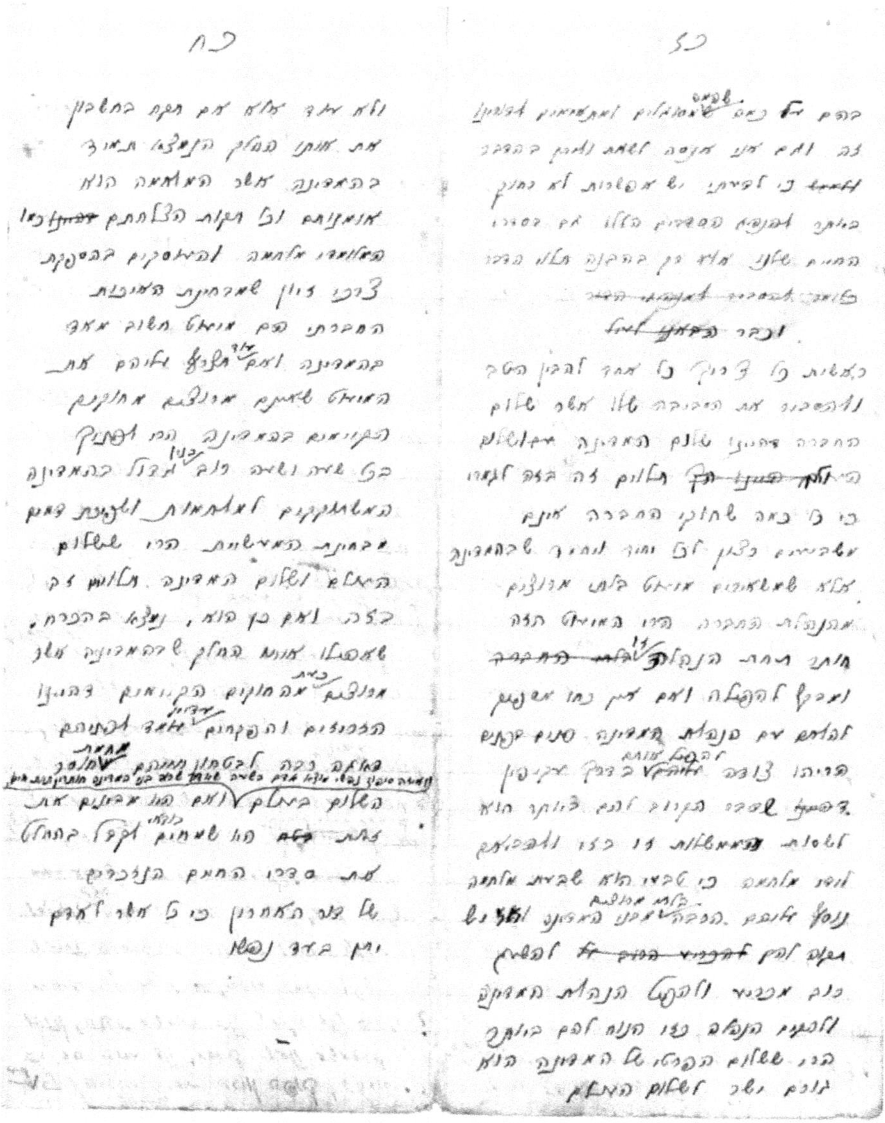

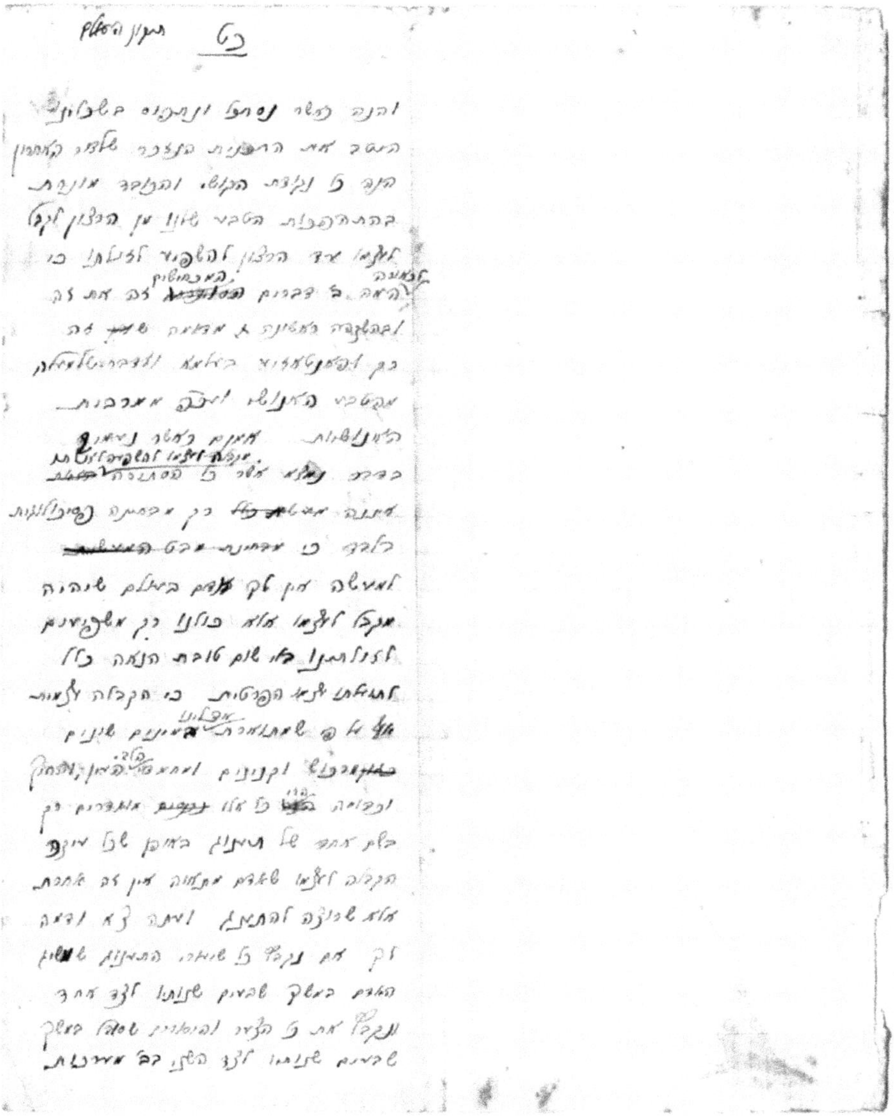

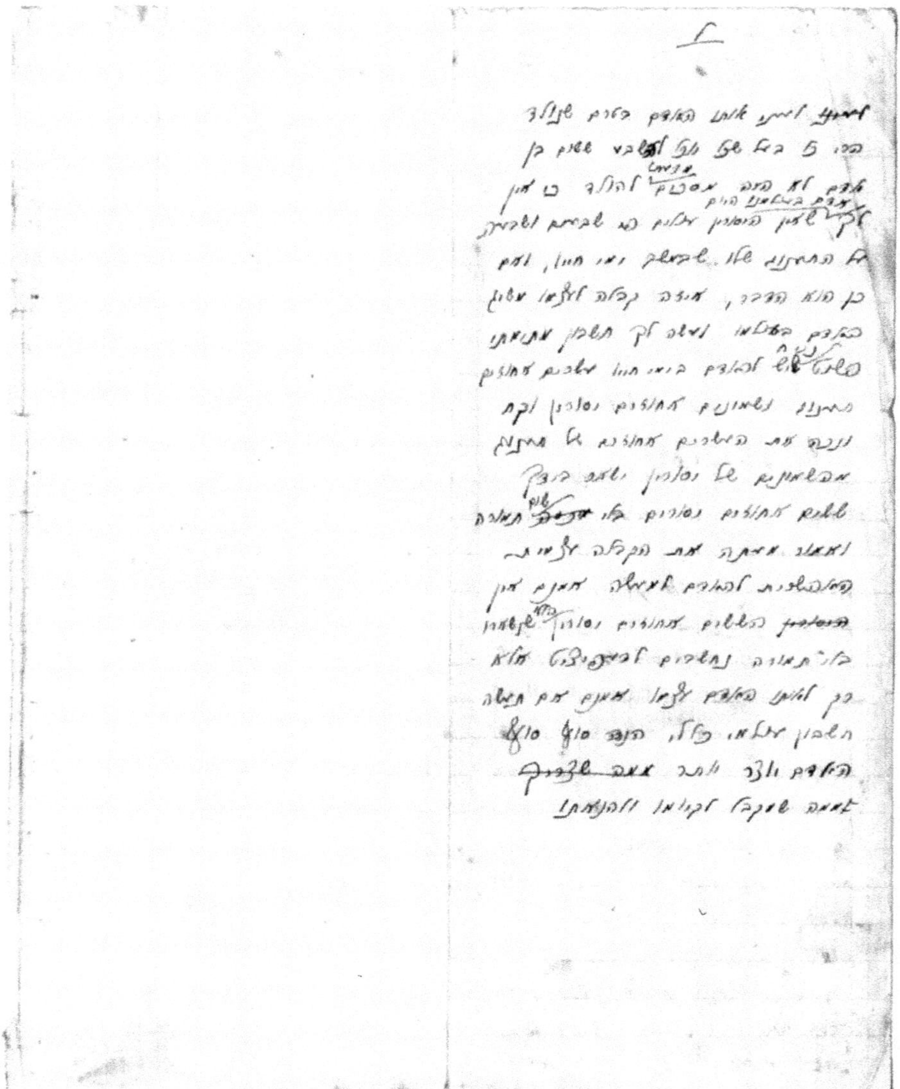

Part Two

One Precept

פרק שני

מצוה אוזת

Successful Work

(8th of ***Nissan*** – 5713)
March 29, 1933

Chapter One:
One Precept

*"He who performs One Precept
tips himself and the whole world
to the scale of merit."*

The Work of the Creator and performing the Precepts are not considered done unless they are For Its Own Sake, which means giving pleasure to [the person's] Maker. At the same time, our sages have established that one should engage in the study of the Torah and in fulfilling the Precepts even [if it is] Not For Its Own Sake, stating that out of doing so Not For Its Own Sake, one will eventually be doing so For Its Own Sake.

עבודה מנצחת

ח׳ ניסן תרצ״ג

פרק ראשון:
מצוה אחת

״עשה מצוה אחת מכריע את
עצמו ואת כל העולם כולו
לכף זכות״.

אין עבודת ה׳ וקיום מצוות זולת לשמה שפירושו לעשות נ״ר נחת רוח ליוצרו אמנם הנהיגו חז״ל חכמינו זכרונם לברכה לעסוק בתורה ומצוות אפי׳ אפילו שלא לשמה מטעם דמי׳ שמתוך שלא לשמה יבוא לשמה.

The subject of Precepts [regarding the relationship] Between a Person and His Friend:

As far as this custom is concerned, for sure one should not question (lit. think) the words of the sages. We should hold on to it [the custom] with all of our might as much as possible. Yet since the outbreak of the War[1], people's patience has become thin, and each and everyone, especially the young, have lost the power to control themselves and for that have become completely rebellious. It has become totally impossible to instill in them the habits of studying the Torah and following the Precepts. Moreover, the whole issue of Not For Its Own Sake, which the spiritual Work of the masses is based on, is not the custom at all these days because respect for the Torah has completely fallen.

Therefore, I have come out with this call to the young Israelites to return to the Work of the Creator and to have faith in Him [even] in a minimal fashion. We do not require of them immediate and total acceptance of the Torah and the Precepts in their entirety, but [simply] that each and every one would, at any rate, accept One Precept. As the sages said: " "Habakkuk [the prophet] came and summed them [the precepts] all in one: 'A righteous person lives by his faith.'" And even if a person says that he will fulfill all the Precepts of the Torah, except for one [he is like a servant who rebels against his master (Rabenu Yona, *Shaarei Teshuva* 6)] this refers to individuals who have become perfected and are now performing the Precepts For Its Own Sake. But before reaching that perfection—when the whole point of this [spiritual] Work is nothing but an exercise and training so that it will bring the individual to do so For Its Own Sake—the loss is not so great between him who fulfills it in whole or in part.

---

1. World War II

ענין מצות בין אדם לחבירו:

והנה מנהג הזה ודאי שאין להרהר אחרי ד׳חז״ל דברי חז״ל ועד כמה שאפשר להחזיק בו אנו מחזיקים בו בכל כחנו אמנם אחר פרוץ המלחמה שנחלשה הסבלנות שכאו׳א שכל אחד ואחד ובעיקר שהצעירים אבדו כח למשול בעצמם וע״ז ועל זה פרקו עול לגמרי ואי אפשר בשום אופן להרגילם בתו׳מצ בתורה ומצוות ולא עוד שכל ענין שלא לשמה שעליו הי׳ מבססים את עבדות ההמונים אינו נהוג כלל בזמן הזה כי נפלה כבוד התורה

וכי ע׳כ על כן באתי בהכרזה זאת לצעירי בי״ בני ישראל לשוב לעבודת הש״י השם יתברך ולאמונתו באופן מקצתי: שאין אנו דורשים מהם תיכף קבלת תומ׳צ תורה ומצוות בשלימות אלא כאו׳א כך אחד ואחד יקבל עכ״פ על כל פנים מצוה אחת כמ׳ש כמו שאמרו חז״ל: בא חבקוק והעמידן על אחת צדיק באמונתו יחי׳ ואע׳פ ואף על פי שהאומר אקיים כל התורה חוץ מדבר אחד וכו׳ [הרי זה כעבד המורד ברבו. (שערי תשובה, רבנו יונה ו׳)] הנה זה אמור בשלימים שכבר עושים המצוות לשמה אמנם בטרם שבאים לשלימות הזה אשר כל העסק בעבודה אינה אלא בחי׳ בחינת הרגל והכשר כדי שמיתוכה יבוא לשמה אז אין ההפסד גדול כ׳כ כל כך במקיימה כולה או מקצתה.

And therefore, I say that the first and only Precept that would be a safe [choice] for one who wishes to achieve [the level of] For Its Own Sake is to take a commitment to work not for his own need except for the minimum requirements to live, that is to say, to the point of providing only for his own existence. And the rest of the time, he should be working for the community, helping the depressed and the ill and every creature in the world who needs benefit, rescue or any help.

Serving people according to the Precepts of the Creator:

This Precept [about serving people] has two virtues: One is that every young person will understand what he is doing because this work is agreed upon and approved by people from all over the world; and the second is that it is possible that this Precept is a better instrument to bring us [closer] to keeping the Torah and the Precepts For Its Own Sake rather than performing all 613 Precepts if they are done out of self-love. Since preparation is in itself part of the goal. In preparing himself to work for other people, [a person] acts for others and for their benefit and not for his own self. And then [it follows that] he will slowly and gradually be prepared to fulfill the Precepts of the Creator according to the desired condition, that is, for the sake of the Creator and not for his own benefit. Ultimately, of course, the purpose should be to fulfill the Precepts of the Creator.

The part of the Torah that deals [with the relationship] Between a Person and His Friend:

There are two parts to the Torah: One dealing [with the relationship] Between a Person and the Creator, and one dealing [with the relationship] Between a Person and his Friend. Therefore, I am calling on you anyhow to engage with and accept everything that pertains to the relationship Between a Person and his Friend, and eventually you will also complete it with whatever pertains [to the relationship] Between a Person and the Creator.

וע׳כ ועל כן אני אומר שמצוה ראשונה והיחידה שתהא יותר בטוחה להחפץ לבא לשמה הוא לקבל על עצמו שלא לעבוד לצורך עצמו זולת במינימום ההכרחי לחיות בהם דהיינו בדיוק עד לידי סיפוק קיומו בלבד ושאר הזמן יעבוד בשביל הצבור להושיע נדכאים וחולים ולכל בריה שבעולם שצריכה ישועה וסתם הטבה.

לשמש לבריות ע׳פ על פי **מצות הש״ת:**

ובמצוה זו יש ב׳ מעלות האחת אשר כל צעיר יבין אשר עושה מפני שעבודה זו היא מוסכמת ומאושרת מכל בני העולם והשנית הוא מפני שיכול להיות אשר מצוה זו היא מכשיר יותר טוב לבא לקיום תורה ומצוות לשמה, מקיום כל התרי׳ג 613 מצוות בשביל אהבה עצמית בשביל שההכנה הוא ממין המטרה כי כהרגיל את עצמו לעבוד לבריות הריהו עושה לאחרים ולטובתם ולא לעצמו וא׳כ ואם כן לאט לאט יוכשר לעשות מצות השם ג׳כ גם כן בתנאי הנרצה דהיינו לטובת הבורא ית׳ ולא לטובת עצמו - וכמובן אשר הכונה צריכה להיות בשביל קיום מצות הש״י .

חלק התורה שבין אדם לחבירו:

באופן שב׳ חלקים בתורה: הנוגע בין אדם למקום, והנוגע בין אדם לחבירו. ועכ׳ ועל כן אני קורא אתכם עכ׳פ על כל פנים לעסוק ולקבל מה שבין אדם לחברו וסוף סוף תשלימו גכ׳ גם כן במה שנוגע לבין אדם למקום.

Speech, thought, action:

The [spiritual] Work, whatever its form may be, should include thought, speech, and action. The subject of practically fulfilling the One Precept has already been clarified, which is that one would commit himself to dedicating all his free time to benefit all created beings in the world. The issue of thought is most important in this Precept, more so than in the special Precepts [regarding the relationship] Between a Person and the Creator, because [when we talk about] the Precepts Between a Person and the Creator,the action itself proves that the intention is for the sake of his Maker, since the action would not have occurred had it not been for Him.

Indeed, the [Precepts] Between a Person and his Friend are justified in and of themselves based on the dictates of human conscience, and if they are performed from this point of view, clearly nothing will be done, meaning that the actions do not bring [the person] closer to the Creator and to doing the Work really For Its Own Sake. Therefore, each and every one must think in his mind that he is doing this [caring for the others] only in order to give pleasure to his Maker and to establish an affinity with His ways: Just as [the Creator] is compassionate, so should we be compassionate; just as He always bestows good onto others, so should we; and so on.

And this affinity, along with doing good deeds, will slowly bring [the person] closer to the Creator in a way that his Form would be made equal to spirituality and holiness. Then [the person] would be transformed into a negative template, like a stamp, and would be made fit for receiving the true Supernal abundance.

And speech is [a matter of] praying with the mouth during the Work and at set times, so that the Creator will grant [a person the merit] to transform his heart from receiving to sharing. It also means contemplating the Torah as well as [other] matters that bring about this transformation.

דבור מחשבה מעשה:

העבודה מאיזה מין שתיהי' צריכה להכלל במחשבה דיבור מעשה והנה ענין מצוה אחת בחלקה המעשי כבר ניתבאר שהוא שיקבל על עצמו שכל שעת הפנאי שלו יהי' מוקדש לתועלת בריות העולם. וענין המחשבה הוא ענין עקרי במצוה זו יותר מבמצוות המיוחדות בין אדם למקום כי אותם שבין אדם למקום, הרי המעשה בעצמו מוכיחה על הכונה לשם יוצרו כי אין שום מקום לאותו המעשה זולתו ית'

אמנם באותם שבין אדם לחבירו אשר מוצדקים מתוך עצמם מתוך מצפון האנושי המחייבתם ואם יעשה מנקודת השקפה הזאת ודאי שלא יעשה כלום כלומר שהמעשים לא יביאוהו לידי קרבת הש"ת ולידי עבודה לשמה ממש אשר ע'כ על כן צריך כאוא' כל אחד ואחד לחשוב במחשבתו שעושה כל אלה רק בשביל לעשות [נחת] רוח ליוצרם ולהתדמות לדרכיו מה הוא רחום אף אנו מרחמים מה הוא משפיע תמיד טובות אף אנו כן וכו'

וענין הדימוי הזאת בצרוף עם המעשים הטובים לאט לאט יקרבהו להש"ת באופן שיושוה צורתו לרוחניות וקדושה שאז יתהפך כחומר חותם ויוכשר לקבלת שפע העליונה האמתית.

וענין הדיבור הוא תפלה בפה בשעת העבודה ובזמנים קבועים שיזכהו הש"ת להפוך לבו מקבלה להשפעה וכן להגות בתורה ובענינים המביאים התהפכות הזה .

I only write about things that are within my comprehension:

Regarding Personal Divine Providence, I understand that there is a difference between [Providence] in spiritual matters and [Providence] in physical matters. In physical matters, Providence is general, while in spiritual matters—that is, the spiritual gifts that are ready [to be given] to each person according to his comprehension—are under total and complete Providence for each and every individual, up to the minutest details, to such precision that the human eye would tire examining them.

Personal Providence:

Because physical and spiritual matters are intertwined (lit. enclothing each other) and profoundly connected down to every last instance, it would be logical to deduce that even physical matters are subject to personal Providence. But because up until now, you have not yet come to know precisely the various connections where spirituality and physicality meet with each other, therefore, you are not able to conceive of Physical Providence, which is a very reasonable assumption. In any event, I am not deciding anything on this matter because my mandate is to write and discuss only that which I see with my own eyes and reach with my own hands and not from theoretical statements, and I have no right to express assumptions [that come only] from my own mind.

Giving pleasure to his Maker unknowingly:

We should never hope that there will come a time when the world will be so evolved that everyone could start the Work of the Creator [at the level of] For Its Own Sake. Rather, as it has always been and still is today and will always be, everyone who fulfills the Work of the Creator must begin [to do so by] becoming engaged with this Work Not For Its Own Sake. And from this, he will achieve [the level of] For Its Own Sake. Indeed, this beginning [For Its Own Sake] is not limited by time but depends on those who prepare it,

איני כותב אלא מה שבהשגתי:

בדבר ההשגחה הפרטיות השגתי בהפרש בין גשמיות לרוחניות אשר הגשמיות מושגח בכללות אמנם הרוחניות כלומר השפעות הרוחניות המוכנות לכל אדם לפי השגתו הרי המה מושגחים לכל פרט ופרט בתכלית ההשגחה המפורטת בקטנטנות מדויק כזה אשר עין אדם ילאה לעמוד עליו.

השגחה פרטיות:

אמנם מתוך שהגשמיות והרוחניות מלובשים זה בזה ומקושרים זב"ז זה בזה לכל מקריהם א"כ אם כן אפשר להסיג מתוך שכל העיוני אשר גם הגשמיות מושגחה בהשגחה פרטיות אלא מתוך שעד הנה עוד לא ידעת בדיוק כל מיני הקשרים אשר הגשמיות והרוחניות יפגשו זה בזה ע"כ על כן לא תוכל להשיג את השגחה הגשמית והוא סברה מקובלת מאוד אולם בין כך ובין כך איני מחליט על ענין זה כלום כי חוקי לכתוב ולהודיע רק מה שאני רואה בשתי עיני ומשיג בשתי ידי ולא מפי משפטים עיוניים ואין לי הצדק לומר סברות מדעתי.

עשיית נ"ר נחת רוח ליוצרו שלא מדעתו:

לעולם אין לקוות על איזה זמן שיתפתח העולם באופן שיוכלו להתחיל את עבודות הש"ת בה"לשמה" אלא כמאז כן היום וכן תמיד מוכרח כל עובד ה' להתחיל בעסק העבודה שלא לשמה אשר מתוכה יבוא אל הלשמה אמנם תחילת הזה אינו מוגבל בזמן אלא בהמכשירים אותו וכפי שליטתו על לבו של עצמו וע"כ ועל כן רבים חללים נפלו ויפלו על שדה העסק שלא לשמה וימותו בלי חכמה

and on his control over his own heart. This is why many casualties have fallen and will yet fall on the battlefield of this issue of Not For Its Own Sake and they will die unwisely. And yet their reward is very great because the mind of a human being is not capable of appreciating how valuable and precious giving pleasure to his Maker is. And even if it [giving pleasure to his Maker] is done by a person who does not fulfill this condition [For Its Own Sake], nevertheless, because he is not fit to do otherwise, he still gives pleasure to his Maker, although [in this case,] this is called "unknowingly."

A prophetic truth in a physical parameter:

Since this is the ultimate certainty, therefore abundance of prophesy must be received by those combinations of letters that fit exactly according to the spirit of the beginners. Meaning that their benefit should be obvious for the personal issues of his generation. Only then can the Word of the Creator be accepted by that generation, in the form of Not For Its Own Sake, since the Creator did not prepare them any differently, as mentioned above. Therefore, this is a sign of a True Prophet, whose prophecy completely fits in for the benefit of the physical success of the people of his generation as is said in the Torah: "And what [other] great nation is there that has statutes and ordinances as righteous as all this law which I set before you this day?" (Deuteronomy 4:8) because the proximity of the physical success validates their truthfulness, since eventually it was undoubtedly the gateway in, as mentioned above.

The 613 Precepts from the aspect of Holy Names:

They are the subject of personal Providence. For anyone who comes close to receiving the Divine abundance. They must go through all these steps, not one of which can be missed. Therefore, those who are perfected pursue them with all their mind and spirit in order to fulfill them completely all the way to their physical branches, according to the secret of the verse: "In every place where I cause My Name to be remembered, I will come to you and bless you." (Exodus 20:24)

ועכ"ז ועם כל זה שכרם גדול מאד כי אין מחשבתו של אדם מסוגל להעריך אותו היקר והערך של עשיית נ"ר נחת רוח ליוצרו ואפי' ואפילו בעושה שלא על תנאי זה מ'מ מכל מקום מתוך שאינו ראוי באופן אחר עושה ג'כ נ"ר גם כן נחת רוח ליוצרו וזה נק' נקרא אמנם שלא מדעתו.

אמת נבואי במודד גופני:

וכיון שכן הוא ודאי המוחלט ע"כ על כן שפע הנבואי מוכרח להתקבל באותם הצירופי אותיות אשר מותאמים לגמרי לרוח המתחילים כלומר שיהיו תועלתם גלוי לענינים העצמיים של הדור שלו כי רק אז מובטחה דבר ה' להתקבל על הדור בהדרך של שלא לשמה: שהבורא ית' לא הכין אותם באופן אחר כנ'ל וע'כ ועל כן זהו סימן של נביא אמת אשר נבואתו מותאמה ביותר לתועלת ההצלחה הגופניית של בני דורו וכמ'ש וכמו שכתוב בתורה "ומי גוי גדול אשר לו משפטים טובים וישרים וכו' (דברים ד', ח') כי קרבת ההצלחה הגופנית יאשר את אמיתותם כי סוף סוף הוא פתח הכניסה בהחלט כנ'ל.

התרי"ג 613 מצוות בבחי" בבחינת שמות קדושים:

הם ענין השגחה פרטיות לכל המתקרב לקבלת שפע האלקי שמוכרחים לעבור עליו כל הסדרים האלה איש מהם לא נעדר וע'כ ועל כן השלימים נוהרים אחריהם בכל נפשם ומאודם לקיימם עד לענפיהם הגשמיים בסו"ה בסוד הכתוב: "בכל מקום אשר אזכיר את שמי אבוא אליך וברכתיך".

The Wisdom of Truth:

Those before me have gone deeply into details while I have chosen a more general path, because in my opinion, it is more appropriate for divinity to be clothed with eternal letter-combinations, which will never be subject to change. What I mean to say is that their physical success will also not be subject to change at any place and at any time. This is why my words are limited, and for the same reason, I was also forced to express spirituality in a general manner. On the other hand, however, I chose to explain, to the very minutest detail, all the features and the spiritual combinations that have no source or origin other than this rule, i.e., the purity of receiving. And because I am speaking of spiritual details without being clothed in any physical combinations, it would greatly benefit the development of comprehension. And this wisdom is called the Wisdom of Truth.

Mistakes or lies can never happen in prophecy:

How can a mistake creep into the Light of the Truth that originates from the Creator? Rather, [His Truth] surely is like the rain and the snow that comes down from Heaven to Earth and do not return until they have accomplished what they were sent for. Furthermore, there is a...

Long and short road in prophecy.

Of course, there are still distinctions between the prophets who receive [messages]; one is not as excellent as the other, since this greatness or smallness can be seen in the degree of preparation of that prophet. Thus, the lesser [prophet], inevitably because of lack of excellent preparation, causes the course of the Light that comes to him to deviate, so much so that it might be possible to say about him that some mistakes mixed in, except there is the iron rule that the Light of prophecy does not make any mistake as mentioned before. Yet because of his smallness, he attracts to himself a greater number of letter-combinations, which is a greater number of channels and Vessels, until he achieves the prophecy.

חכמת האמת:

הקודמים הכניסו א׳ע את עצמם לפרטים ואני בחרתי דרך כללי כי לדעתי מותאם יותר לענין אלקי להלבישו בצירופי אותיות נצחיות אשר לא יקבלו שינוי לעולם רצוני לומר שהצלחתם הגופני גכ׳ גם כן לא יקבל שינוי בשום מקום ובשום זמן ולכן דברי מוגבלים וגם את הרוחניות הוכרחתי משום זה להביע בדרך כלל אמנם תחת זה בחרתי לבאר כל הפרטים והצירופים הרוחניים עד לפרטי פרטיות אשר אין להם מוצא ומקור אחר זולת מפי כלל הזה דהיינו טהרת הקבלה ומתוך שאני מדבר מהפרטים הרוחנים בלי הלבשה בצירופים גשמיים יועיל הדבר הרבה להתפתחות ההשגה וחכמה זו נק׳ נקראת חכמת האמת.

לא יארע טעות או שקר בהנבואה:

כי באור האמת הנובע מהשי׳ת איך יפול בו טעות אלא ודאי כמו הגשם והשלג היורד משמים אל האדמה ושמה לא ישוב עד שיצליח לאשר שלחתיו אמנם עכ׳ז עם כל זה....

יש דרך ארוכה וקצרה בהנבואה:

כי ודאי שיש הבחן עכ״פ על כל פנים בהנביאים המקבלים שאין אחד מעולה כחבירו ממש שגדלות וקטנות הזאת נבחן כפי ההכנה שבאותו הנביא והנה הקטן בהכרח מטעם חוסר ההכנה המעולה מפיל איזה נטיה במהלך האור הנשפע אליו שהיה יתכן לומר עליו אשר נתערב איזה טעות אלמלא החוק הברזל אשר אור הנבואה אינו מקבל טעות כנ״ל אמנם קטנותו הזאת גורם אליו ריבוי בצירופי אותיות שהוא ריבוי צינורות וכלים עד שיבוא לו הנבואה לכדי השגה.

Prophetic success is [measured by] speed:

Even though ultimately all the truth in the prophecy is revealed with the desired success, still this [lesser] prophet has caused [the prophecy to take] a longer road to the people to whom he was sent with his prophecy. This is unlike the greater [prophet] whose preparation is more complete, and [who] therefore does not experience any deviation when he receives the prophecy from the Creator. For this reason, he does not use a greater number of channels and Vessels. Therefore, his prophecy is clear and concise, and is easily and quickly adopted by those to whom he was sent.

It is possible that the lesser [prophet] would succeed more than the greater:

In addition to what has been said above, it is possible that the lesser of the prophets would be more successful with regard to a speedy [acceptance] of his prophecy than a prophet who is the greatest among prophets. This is because he [the lesser prophet] is supported by the revelations of prophets who preceded him and opened the way. Of course, much depends on the development of those who listen to His [the Creator's] words. This is because a shorter and clearer message requires a more advanced and more prepared generation to understand it. And with these two additions given to the lesser [prophet], he can surely succeed more extensively than the greater one.

The speed would indicate the number of those who would reach completion by him:

Suppose, for example, that his prophecy is sent to 100 people: If it is going through a long way, it can bring to completion only one person in a generation, and if so, then the duration of his prophecy will be 100 years. If he takes a shorter route, clearly he will bring 30 or 50 people to completion in a generation, and obviously his prophecy will be completed within only a few years.

הצלחה הנבואי הוא המהירות:

באופן שאע"פ שאף על פי שסוף סוף מתגלה כל האמת שבהנבואה בהצלחה הרצויה מ"מ מכל מקום גרם הנביא [לנבואה לעבור] דרך ארוכה [יותר] אל האנשים שאליהם נשלח בנבואתו משא'כ מה שאין כן הגדול אשר הכנתו יותר שלימה הרי לא יארע לו שום נטיה בעת קבלת נבואתו מהשי'ת ומחמת זה לא ירבה בצנורות וכלים וע'כ וכל כן נבואתו ברורה וקצרה ומקובלים בנקל ובמהירות לאותם שאליהם נשלח.

אפשר שהקטן יצליח יותר מגדול

ומלבד האמור יתכן שהקטן שבנביאים יצליח בנבואתו כלומר בענין המהירות כנ'ל, יותר מנביא היותר גדול שבהנביאים והוא מטעם שנסמך על הגילויים של הנביאים הקודמים שפינו לו הדרך ומובן שגם תלוי בהתפתחות השומעים את דבריו י'ת כי לדברים קצרים וברורים צריכים לדור יותר מפותח שיהיו מוכשרים להבינו ומכח ב' הוספות האלו אם יספחו להקטן יכול להצליח ודאי באין ערוך יותר מהגדול.

המהירות יורה ריבוי הנשלמים על ידו:

כלומר אם למשל נבואתו נשלח למאה אנשים אז אם עושה דרך ארוכה אינו משלים רק לחד בדרא וא'כ ואם כן ימשיך זמן נבואתו מאה שנים ואם עושה דרך קצרה מובן שמשלים שלשים או חמשים בדור וממילא נשלם נבואתו באיזה שנים בלבד.

The secret of prophecy throughout the generations:

Moses received the Torah and the religion for all the generations, and no prophet is allowed to innovate anything. Yet at the same time, prophetic ability is given to him for a certain time period. This is supported by what is written: "The Lord, your God, will raise up for you a prophet like me from among you, from your brethren—to him you shall heed." (Deuteronomy 18:15) Had Moses' prophecy been sufficient for eternity, why should the Creator bring forward more prophets like him? But surely his prophecy is good only for a certain time, and when this time is over, the Creator sends another prophet to continue and complete His Will. Of course, this prophet is not allowed to bring any new ideas or to take anything away because that would mean that the previous prophet was not perfect, heaven forbid. The Word of the Creator always comes in its highest and most complete form, according to the secret of the verse: "I am the first and I am the last." (Isaiah 44:6) So [the later prophet's] sole duty is to continue [to deliver] the same prophecy to the generations who do not deserve anymore to receive from the first one. And the last prophet is the secret of the Messiah, which means that he [the Messiah] is completing all the others. Surely he is not allowed to add or delete anything. Rather, his success would be greater; that is to say, the entire generation would be prepared to accept his words and to come to completion through him. This is because of the two reasons mentioned earlier: either because of his greatness, or because of the level of preparedness of the people of his generation (as mentioned earlier), or because of them both.

The principle of the prophetic success:

The extending of the Exalted Light to those dwelling below. And [the prophet] who is able to bring [the Light] to the lowest [level] is the one who is most successful. Now the matter of high and low is valued by the spirit and physical benefit because the physicality that is achieved through prophecy is its hand *[Tefillin]* box that was given to be grasped by human beings. And it is known that the main issue in the Work is the first grasp.

סוד הנבואה שבדורות:

אע'פ שמרעה"ש אף על פי שמשה רבנו עליו השלום הוא מקבל התורה והדת בשביל כל הדורות עד שאין הנביא רשאי לחדש דבר עכ"ז עם כל זה אין נבואתו ניתן לו אלא לזמן וע"ז ועל זה מעיד הכתוב: נביא כמוני יקים לך ה' אלקיך אליו תשמעון ואם נבואת משה בלבדו היה מספיק לנצחיות למה לו להשי'ת להקים עוד נביאים כמותו אלא ודאי שאין נבואתו מועילה אלא לזמן מסוים שבכלות הזמן שולח השי'ת נביא אחר להמשיך ולהשלים חפץ השי'ת אמנם ודאי שאינו רשאי לחדש דבר או לגרוע דא'כ הי' בחי' שאם כן היה בחינת חסרון בנביא הקודם ח'ו חס ושלום אלא דבר ה' תמיד בכל השלימות בסו'ה בסוד הכתוב אני ראשון ואני אחרון אלא כל תפקידו הוא להמשיך אותו הנבואה לאותם הדורות שכבר אינם ראוים לקבל מהראשון והנביא האחרון ה'ס הוא סוד משיח כלומר המשלים על כולם אמנם ודאי ג'כ גם כן שאינו רשאי להוסיף או לגרוע אלא שהצלחתו יהי' יותר גדולה דהיינו שכל הדור יוכשר לקבל את דבריו ונשלמים על ידו והוא מב' טעמים הנ'ל או מחמת גדלותו, או מחמת הכשר בני דורו כנ'ל או מחמת שניהם.

עיקר ההצלחה הנבואיי:

הוא להמשיך אור העליון עד לדרי מטה והמורידו ביותר למטה הוא המצליח ביותר וענין מעלה ומטה נבחן ברוח ובטובה גופניות כי הגופניות המושג על ידי הנבואה הוא הבית יד שלה הניתן לאחיזה לבני העולם: ונודע שעיקר נקודת הכובד בהעבודה הוא האחיזה הראשונה.

General power and individual power:

Their unity is the secret of the unification of the Creator and the *Shechinah* (Divine Presence). The individual power is the [the power of] forbidding to receive down to the minimum; the general force is increasing the amount of sharing with all one's heart and soul.

כח כללי וכח פרטי:

אחודם ה'ס הוא סוד **יחוד קוב'ה** קודשא בריך הוא **ושכינתא** (הדקוש ברוך הוא והשכינה) כח פרטי הוא איסור הקבלה עד למינימום כח כללי הוא ריבוי ההשפעה עד בכל מאודו ונפשו.

Chapter Two: Cleaving

The basis of the Torah and Cleaving:

Delight and wisdom are surely extended from His Essence, and everyone who receives, in the spiritual sense, does not receive anything except through Cleaving [to the Creator]. And whoever is more cleaved and is more close, his delight and his wisdom are more abundant. And whoever is completely separated [from the Creator] will necessarily dwell in plenty of sorrow and stupidity. Indeed, we need to understand…

…what does Cleaving mean?

To begin with, [Cleaving means] knowing your own self. I can tell you that this ["self"] is no more and no less than the Desire to Receive that you feel within yourself. And this [Desire to Receive] is all the difference between those who are alive and those who are dead—that when one has lost the Desire to Receive, he is called dead, just like a broken vessel. Indeed, in terms of His Essence, the aspect of Desire to Receive is evident only through Sharing because He has no one to receive from; nevertheless, through His actions, we conclude that He has a Desire to Share, to produce and love between friends.

Closeness between spiritual bodies:

This you can learn from the [example of] closeness between physical bodies—that at the time of their closeness to one another, the surpluses of one of them enters into [and completes] the shortages of the other. This is [also what happens] between countries and the like. Indeed, closeness between spiritual bodies is a matter of Similarity of Form, just as love is a similarity of form and opinions,

פרק שני:
דביקות

יסוד התורה והדביקות:

ענין העונג והחכמה נמשך ודאי מעצמותו ית׳ וכל המקבל בדרך רוחני אינו מקבל רק בדרך הדביקות וכל הדבוק יותר ומקורב יותר יהי׳ תענוגו וחכמתו יותר בשפע והנפרד לגמרי ישרה בהכרח ברוב צער וטפשות אמנם צריך להבין ....

...עניין דביקות מהו?

ומתחילה הכר את אני שלך ואומר לך שאינו לא פחות ולא יותר מדבר הרצון לקבל שאתה מרגיש בך ובזה כל ההפרש מחיים להמתים שבאבדת הרצון לקבל נק׳ נקרא מת כמו כלי קבלה שנשברה אמנם בעצמותו ית׳ לא נבחן ענין רצון לקבל זה רק בדרך השפעה כי אין לו ממי שיקבל אולם מתוך פעולותיו אנו יכולין להחליט שיש לו רצון להשפיע להולדה ואהבת רעים.

קירוב גופין רוחניים

ועתה צא ולמד מדביקות גופין גשמים שעודפות של האחד נכנסים בשעת קרבתם זל״ז זה לזה אל הגרעונות של משנהו שהם המדינות וכדומה אמנם ענין הקרבה בגופים רוחניים הוא ענין שיווי צורה כמו שהאהבה הוא השואת הצורה והדעות והשנאה הוא להיפך - ולפיכך בעת אשר תבטל את הרצון לקבל שבך הרי אתה מקרב

while hate is the opposite. Consequently, the moment you cancel the Desire to Receive within you, you bring your spiritual body closer to His [the Creator's] Essence because you are totally in the aspect of sharing with others, which is the [equivalent of] giving pleasure to your Maker. This is the intention that you want to fulfill so that you will be prepared for the ultimate purpose of Creation. Therefore, when this closeness reaches the desired level and is well measured, then you will find yourself Cleaving to His Essence. And according to the degree [of Cleaving], His surpluses will enter your deficits, meaning to the pleasure and wisdom that are engraved in your deficits because of your lowliness.

The deficits are the main issue:

Here we are not dealing with surpluses, only with deficits. Therefore, it is not enough and not sufficient that you will share as much to other human beings as He [the Creator] does, because then you would not have deficits to [allow you to] become unified with Him, as in physical Cleaving. This would not be the case if you will only train yourself….

...to share with His Names:

This intention repeatedly creates great emptiness in you because you do not know before whom you are performing the labor; and the power of your quest is the empty space in your deficits, which is opened for you. Because it is through there [the opening] that the matter of the matching—between [the Creator's] surpluses and your deficits at the time of Cleaving—occurs, and then they unite and shall never part for all eternity.

את גופך הרוחני לעצמותו ית' כי כולך בבחי' בבחינת השפעה לזולתך אתה נמצא שהוא השפעת נ"ר נחת רוח ליוצרך שאתה רוצה לקיים הכונה כדי שתהיה מוכשר לתכלית הבריאה ולפיכך בהגיע קרבה זאת לשיעור הרצוי ומשוער היטב אז נמצאת דבוק בעצמותו ית' וכפי שיעור זה יכנסו עדפות שלו בגרעונותיך דהיינו העונג והחכמה החרותים בך בגרעונות מסבת שפלותך.

הגרעונות הם עיקר:

וכאן אין לנו עסק בעודפות רק בגרעונות וע'כ ועל כן אינו די ואינו מספיק שתשפיע לבני אדם כמותו ית' כי אז לא תהיה לך גרעונות להלכד עמו כמו בדבקות הגשמי- משא'כ מה שאין כן אם תרגיל רק...

...להשפיע לשמותיו ית':

הרי כונה זאת חוזרת וגורע אותך מאוד מחמת כי לא תדע לפני מי אתה עמל וכח הביקוש שבך הוא החלל שבגרעונותיך הנפתח לך שדרך שם נעשה ענין זווג עודפותיו ית' אל הגרעונות ההם בשעת הדביקות ואז יתלכדו ולא יתפרדו לנצח.

Similarity of opinions is the aspect of the "reality of lovers," and injecting the surpluses into other people's deficits is the existence:

We need to understand that everything has an aspect of the reality [of lovers] and the existence of the reality. And surely we need to start with the reality that is referred to as "loving one another." Yet even though this reality appears in front of us, we still need to nourish it to ensure its existence because the success of this reality depends on this existence. And this is what we said earlier: That one should renounce the aspect of receiving for his own needs because with this, one gives birth to the reality of lovers through Similarity of Form. [Once this reality is born,] it is necessary to maintain it, and this can be made possible by sharing with others, since all are being brought into play by Him. Common sense dictates that everyone who performs an action would have pleasure from the success of his actions, and this includes all creatures. And so all the [domains]—Inanimate, Vegetation, Animal and Human—are needed together. Yet for sure, the law of priority and selection applies here.

Preparation of the deficits for His Surpluses:

Here these deficits are still non-existent in [the person's] development, and we need to create them. Indeed, these [deficits] also develop through sharing with others, which means that if your sole intention is to Give Pleasure to your Maker, then a need would develop within you to know for whom you are performing this labor; and He keeps on creating more and more lack within you until it reaches the degree that is desired and designed by Him.

השוואת הדעות הוא בחי' בחינת "מציאות אוהבים" והכנסות העודפות בגרעונות חבירו הוא קיומם:

וצריך להבין שכל דבר נבחן במציאות וקיום המציאות שודאי מתחילה צריכים להמציאות שנק' שנקרא אוהבים זל"ז זה לזה. אמנם הגם שנגלה לענינו זה המציאות צריכים עוד ליתן לו מזונות לקיום אשר הצלחת המציאות תלוי בקיום הזה וזה שאמרנו שצריכים להנזר מבחי' מבחינת הקבלה לצרכי עצמו ובזה נולד ובא מציאת האוהבים ע'פ על פי השואת הצורה אמנם לקיום זה המציאות צריכים וזהו יתכן בהשפעה לזולתך היות שהם כולם נפעלים הימנו ית' והשכל מחייב שכל פועל יש לו נר' נחת רוח בהצלחת פעולותיו שהם הבריות כולם וביחד צריך כל הדצח"ם דומם, צומח, חי, מדבר אמנם ודאי דין הקדם וברירה יש כאן.

הכנת גרעונות לעודפותיו ית':

הנה הגרעונות אלו עדיין אינם קימים בהתפתחות שלו וצריכים להמציאם אמנם גם אלה מתפתחים ע' על ידי השפעה לזולת והיינו אם כל כונתך תהי' רק לעשות נר' נחת רוח ליוצרך ואז יתפתח בך הצורך לידע לפני מי אתה עמל והוא הולך וגורע אותך עד לשיעור הנרצה ומשוער לו ית'.

Chapter Three:
Global Spirituality and Local Spirituality

It has been 12 years now since I started working on a manifesto that will serve as a solid foundation. And for this purpose, after "toiling and finding," I am hereby reading it to you.

What has brought me to this is my great devotion to the idea and because I have assumed in advance, that it is not sustainable without a basis in religion. And there has never been throughout history a major push of the masses—such as nationalism or law and order—without this basis, not to mention the issue of letting go private property. Moreover, we do not have any higher or more exalted concept, and yet this is accepted only by wise people of clear mind and not at all by those of crude materialism and by the masses.

As for them, without private property, they don't find any motive-power for voluntary bodily movement in a direct manner but only in an indirect manner—meaning in a roundabout manner, which is a very weak method for success and is bound to fade away completely. Because through compulsion, not only is their Work incomplete, but also we need supervisors and guards to keep watching over them, at least one for every 100 people. And this here is the crux of the problem (lit. where the dog is buried) because the culture of our generation is not yet high enough that it would give us the one in 100 people who has a heart of wisdom and pure consciousness. And then the guarantor needs to be guaranteed because even the supervisor needs motive-power for the Work of supervision, [which is] something he has not.

In general, I have nothing to offer except for the One Precept whose reward is infinite: True Cleaving, which is described as "No eye has seen a God besides thee." (Isaiah 64:3) And this is the Precept of Work and of sharing with the community, and of adding additional benefit to them on top of any benefit they already enjoy—and the

פרק שלישי:

רוחניות גלובלית ורוחניות מקומית

זה י"ב שנים שאנכי עוסק בעיבוד דעת שישמש בסיס נאמן ולמטרה זו ואחר שיגעתי ומצאתי הנני להשמיע לפניכם .

ומה שהביאני לזה הוא מתוך מסירתי הגדולה להרעיון ומתוך ששיערתי מראש שאיננו כלל בן קימא לעמוד בלי בסיס דתי ואין לנו שום דחיפה המונית בהסטריא בלי בסיס הזה כמו המשפטים והנאציונאליות ואצ"ל ואין צורך לומר ענין ביטול קנין פרטי והגם שאין לנו מושג יותר נשגב ונעלה הימנו ועם זה אינו מקובל רק על חכמי לב ונקיי הדעת ולא כלל לגסי החומר ולהמונים.

ואצלם בלי קנין פרטי לא נמצא להם שום מאטיוו-פאווער לתנועה גופניות רצוניות באורח ישר אלא רק בארח בלתי ישר דהיינו ע"י על ידי עקיפין שהוא עניין חלש להצלחה וסופו להגווע לגמרי כי מלבד שעבודה ע"י על ידי כפיה אינה שלימה הנה עכ"פ על כל פנים צריכים אנו לעומדים על גביהם לשומרים ולמכייפין לכל הפחות אחד על מאה וכאן הכלב קבור כי עדין אין קולטוריזאציע תרבות של דורינו גבוה במדה שיתן חכמי לב ונקיי הדעת אחד אחוז למאה וא"כ ואם כן ערבך ערבא צריך המשגיח צריך שישגיחו עליו כי גם המשגיח צריך למאטיוו-פאווער כח מניע לעבודת ההשגחה וזהו אין לו .

ובכללות אין לי להציע רק מצוה אחת ששכרו אין קץ שהוא דביקות האמיתי שעין לא ראתה אלקים זולתיך והוא המצוה לעבוד ולהשפיע להצבור להוסיף להם תועלת על התועלת - ולפום צערא

Reward will be According to the Effort. And exactly opposite to this, there is only One Sin, which is egoism also in a more narrow sense, meaning that any self-enjoyment is a transgression.

Therefore, anyone who decreases this transgression receives his reward as payment from his Maker. Meaning, that a person should not enjoy anything in this world except to the extent that he shares with the community and with the Creator in order to make the Creator and the people happy. And any drop of enjoyment exceeding this degree is a transgression, and this *Nefesh* (Lower Soul) will be completely severed from human society and would reincarnate as a wild animal (all this unless [the person] atones for the sin) and would be put to work against his will.

And of course, these things [concerning One Precept] have to be in the form of working for the sake of the Creator and not for the community. Meaning that the Creator has provided us with ways to give Him pleasure, He has prepared a community for each individual, and a cardinal rule: That [a person] should serve his community and be useful to them. And the Creator accepts this Work and this Pleasure as if it—the same degree of benefit and Pleasure—was sent directly to Him by members of His world.

Here we need to expand the explanation regarding reward and punishment to the level that fits the masses. But the main point is the necessity of the wise to understand it because only the understanding of the wise leaders establishes and supports the deeds of the masses.

I have worked on them for 12 years until I have managed to edit them with a deeper sense and deeper reasoning than any of the theology and mysticism of all those that came before me, as our eyes shall observe. And in order to declare it thoroughly, you should send to me a group of wise people who are well versed with your system and let them examine and find out.

אגרא לפי הטרחה - השכר ולעומתו יש רק עבירה אחת והוא עגואיזם גם במובן היותר צר דהיינו כל הנאת עצמו הוא עבירה.

וע'כ ועל כן כל מי הממעט בעבירה הזאת נוטל שכרו משלם מבוראו באופן שאסור להנות בעוה"ז בעולם הזה רק בשיעור שיוכל להשפיע להצבור ולהאלוקים שישמח אלקים ואנשים וכל טפה של הנאה העודפת על השעור האמור הוא עבירה וכרת תיכרת הנפש הזה מאומה האנושית ויתגלגל בבהמות השדה (כ"ז כל זה [במקרה] שלא ישוב בתשובה) ויעבודו בו בע"כ בעל כורחו.

וכמובן שהדברים האלו צריכין להיות בצורת עבודת ה' ולא לעבודת צבור אלא באופן שהשי'ת המציא לנו דרך לעשות לו נ"ר נחת רוח וע"כ ועל כן הכין לכל פרט צבור וכלל גדול שישמשם ויועיל להם וה' מקבל את עבודה זו ונ"ר ונחת רוח זה כמו שהגיע ממש אליו ית' אותו שיעור תועלת ונ'ר ונחת רוח מבני עולמו .

וכאן צריכים להרחבת ביאור בשכר ועונש במדה המתאימה להמונים אמנם בעיקר הדבר צריכים להבנת החכמים כי רק הבנת הגדולים מעמדים ומקיימים המעשה אצל ההמונים כנודע

וי'ב שנים עבדתי עליהם עד שהצלחתי לערוך אותם בטעם ובשכל עמוק יותר מכל התאוליגיה ומיסטיק של כל הקודמים כמו שעינינו תחזנה ולהודיע אתו על בוריו עליכם לשלוח אלי קבוצה של חכמי דעת המותאמים לשיטתכם ויבדקו וימצאו

To explain this, I have prepared two approaches: One way follows theoretical theology, as is common up to the present in all matters; and the second way is according to the mysticism, based on things that have been recognized by the wise of yore over the past few thousand years.

And here, events of our time have paved the way so that it is possible to publicize this opinion of mine to the world. I am referring to the various peace associations that have proliferated in the world at the present time. Through this desperate yearning for peace, the world is able to accept my opinion, although I am afraid that they may take this opinion of mine and cover it with cloth of egoism, in which case it would bring a curse rather than a blessing. Therefore, I cannot stray from my initial thoughts because I have labored and written this manifesto only for you. And now it is really like cold water sprinkled on a tired soul, as I can see by your present state.

In regard to financial issues and all that pertains to material property, it is mandatory not to make changes on any account, for there is no difference between people, between the black and the white and the yellow, between the wise and the foolish. They are all equal, and each is obliged to give to the world as much as he or she can, receiving what he or she needs without prejudice or favoritism. This is an absolute law.

As for spiritual [and intellectual] properties that do no harm to the economy or to material happiness—namely, united ideals and legalities, as well as political reasoning, ethics, and aesthetics—all these should remain national, that is, local. No nation should be forced to forego its customs and preferences as long as it will not harm, at all, the customary straightforward laws of the economy.

In a word, material internationalism should be meticulously maintained, and alongside it, spiritual nationalism should be preserved as long as it does not impact [lit. touch] material internationalism.

ולזה הכינותי ב׳ דרכים דרך א׳ הוא ע׳פ על פי תיאולוגיא העיונית כנוהג עד הנה בכל הדברים ודרך ב׳ הוא ע׳פ על פי מיסטיסיזם המיוסד על דברים מקובלים על חכמים קדמונים זה אלפי שנה.

והנה מאורעות הזמן פינו דרך שאפשר לפרסם דעתי זה לדעת העולם והיינו על אגודות השלום שנתרבו בעולם בעת הזאת וע״י ועל ידי רוב הצפיה לשלום בכליון עינים מסוגלים העולם לקבל דעתי זה עליהם - אמנם ירא אנכי פן ואולי ילבישו על דעתי זה את השמלה של עגואיזם אשר אז תביא קללה תחת ברכה ולפיכך לא אוכל נטות מתחילת מחשבתי אשר לא עבדתי ולא הכינותי דעתי זה רק בשבילכם אשר באמת הוא עתה כמים קרים על נפש עיפה ע׳פ על פי מצבכם העתי.

האופן אשר בעניני הכלכלה וכל קנינים הגשמיים זהו ודאי חיוב מוחלט שלא לשנות בשום פנים שאין שום חילוק בין איש לאיש בין שחור ובין לבן או צהוב, חכמים או כסילים כולם שווים המה כל אחד מחויב ליתן להעולם כמה שיכול ולקבל כמה שצריך בלי שום הפרש יחסים אחרים וזהו חוק מוחלט.

אמנם בקנינים רוחניים שאינם מזיקים להכלכלה ולהאושר הגשמי דהיינו אידיאות דומות ומשפטיות גם הטעם המדיני העתיקא והסטעטיקא כל אלו צריכים להשאר נאציונאליזם כלומר מקומיים ואין לכפות שום אומה או מקום לעבור על מנהגיה וטעמיה באותו השיעור שאינו מזיק כלום לחוקי הכלכלה הישרה המקובלת.

במלה אחת אינטרנאציונליזם גשמי צריך להשמר בכל הדקדוקים ויחד עמה צריך להשמר נאציונאליזם רוחני באותו השיעור שאינו נוגע כלל את האינטרנאציונליזם הגשמי.

My advice, therefore, is that everywhere within your borders, the secular and the religious alike must accept the national and international religion, like I suggested. Whoever transgresses or weakens it is punishable as if he were harming humanity. This is the divine international religion that every human being is ordered to fulfill. Otherwise, he will be uprooted from the World to Come and he will lose both worlds.

Indeed, God allows every nation to keep its religious customs that were received by their great sages; each country according to its preferences and spirit, since undoubtedly they would help any individual country, to its liking. Eventually, [all nations] will be able to completely accept the international religion that is lofty and above them all—the prophetic last word. Whoever denies this principle, his religion is damaged and harmful, and will deserve a severe punishment and should be prevented from this harmful attribute. Yet, a person who accepts our principle will find that his individual religious work becomes acceptable because it is necessary that it be validated in order to finally help the international religion.

In a word, individual religion must be constructed in such a way that it would be just a tool to reach the universal religion. If it becomes known that some countries are damaging again what they have corrected before and the [individual] religion became the most important and ultimate goal, they would be punished and their religion would be completely forbidden by law.

Do not ask what the benefit would be if we start cutting back religions and war is restored. Indeed, God can change any religion; and with a carefully planned design, this international faith can be fully brought into the midst of the masses when God annuls all the additions that the middle class added to the religion for their own benefit. He revealed this to his prophets to ease the work and toil that the middle class deceitfully came up with for their own advantage.

ולפיכך עצתי אשר כל המקומות שבגבולכם כחפשי כדתי מחויבים לקבל את דת המדינה ודת העולמי האינטרנאציונאלי כהצעתי וכל העובר או מחלישה ענוש יענש כמו מזיק לאנושות והוא דת האלקים הבין לאומי שכל בן אדם מצווה עליה שמשום זה יעקר גם מעולם הבא ונמצא אובד ב׳ עולמות

אמנם אלקים מניח לכל אומה לאחוז במינהגיה הדתיים המקובלים אליהם מפי גדוליהם כל מדינה לפי טעמה ורוחה מישום שבלי ספק יעזרו לכל מדינה פרטית בהיותה לטעמיה עד שיוכלו לקבל בשלימות הדת הבין לאומי הגבוה ונעלה על כולנה כי היא מלה האחרונה הנבואי וע׳כ ועל כן הכופר בעיקר הזה נמצא גם דתו מקולקל ומזיק וראוי לענשו קשה ולמונעו מדתו המזיקה אמנם המודה בעיקר שלנו כבר גם עבודת דתו הפרטי נתכשרה להיותה מוכרח להאמת אותה שתעזרה סוף סוף לדת הבין לאומי.

במלה אחת הדת הפרטי מוכרח להתקן בצורה כזו עד שתהיה רק בבח׳ בבחינת מכשיר להגיע להדת הכללי ואם יודע הדבר שאיזה מדינה חזרו וקלקלו התיקונים של הכשרה ועשו דתם לעיקר ולגמר דבר אז ענוש יענשו ויאסרו את דתם לגמרי ע׳פ על פי חוק.

ואין להקשות א׳כ אם כן מהו הרווח אם נבא בקיצוצים על הדתות חזרה המלחמה למקומה אמנם לאלקים מותר לשנות כל דת ובדרך תכנית משוער היטב אפשר להביא את האמונה זו הבין לאומי בתוך ההמונים אשר האלקים ביטל כל התוספות שהוסיפו הבורגנות בתוך הדתות לטובתם וגילה זה לנביאיו למען הקל את היגיעה והעול אשר הבורגנים בדו מלבם לטובתם ברמאות.

Surely there would be some clear-minded among you who would say, "We have already managed to uproot a great amount from the masses. Shall we be messengers now to return ignorance to its place?" Be careful of being extreme. Do not quickly make poor people wealthy both materially and in knowledge. First, we should fix the international economy, using all the tools in our hands since the end justifies the means, especially a sacred, difficult-to-realize goal such as this. After we arrange the economy throughout the world, we can take our time uprooting deviant opinions from the world. First, we need to create healthy bodies; then we can start taking care of good souls for those bodies.

It is a law of nature that one's will is not to be broken because of someone else's will, but only because of one's own will. Even when a weak person surrenders his will to someone more aggressive than him, he does so because of his own desire to protect himself from pain and so forth.

It is a psychological law that there is no will that can be broken while being the only will working and dominating. Whenever anyone's will is broken anywhere in the world, it happens only because its owner has attached another will to it, and when the two wills are standing in the same place, it is inescapable that they will wear and erode each other—and in doing so, their form is blurred and their force is lost.

I am mentioning this because I find that you are not focusing your work on manifesting your goal. On the contrary, you keep adding various [other] things you want, without noticing whether these drain your energy or add confrontations and resistance. This is the greatest evil and history will never forgive you for this crime and malice. So why, in these difficult times, do you fight something that is not directly necessary for your goals? This is nothing but foolishness and lack of attention to your role.

ובטח יהיו נקיי דעת ביניכם לומר אם כבר הספקנו לעקור שיעור גדול מהמונים, נהיה עתה שליחים להחזיר הבערות למקומו אמנם הזהרו ממותרות אין לכם להעשיר את העני בכלכלה ודעת בפעם אחת מתחילה יש לנו לסדר הכלכלה הבין לאומי בכל האמצעים שבידינו כי המטרה מכשירה את האמצעים ובפרט מטרה קדושה וכבדה למעשה כזאת ואחר שנסדר את הכלכלה בכל העולם אז ניקח זמן לעקור דעות עקומות מהעולם מתחילה יש לנו לברא גופים בריאים ואח"ז ואחרי זה נתחיל לדאוג בעד נשמות טובות להגופים ההם .

חוק טבעי הוא שאין רצון נשבר מכח רצון זולתו אלא רק מפני רצון של עצמו ואפי' ואפילו החלש המבטל רצונו מפני התקיף ממנו הוא מחמת רצונו עצמו המגין על עצמו מכאב וכדומה.

וחוק פסיכולוגי הוא שאין שום רצון נשבר בהיותו עומד ושולט לבדו וכל הרצונות שנשברו בעולם לא נשברו רק משום שבעליהם צירפו לו עוד רצון וכששני רצונות עומדים במדור אחד אז לא ימלט שלא ישחקו זה לזה ובזה נטשטשה צורתם ואובדים את כוחן.

והזכרתי זה בשביל שאני מוצא שאינכם מצמצמים את עבודתכם על מטרתכם בלבד להשליטה רק תוסיפו עליה עוד דברים הרצויים לכם מבלי להשגיח כלל אם שואבים את האנערגיע או גם מוסיפים מלחמות והתנגדות כי זהו הרעה היותר גדולה ולעולם לא ימחול לכם ההסטוריא על פשע וזדון הזה כי מה לכם עתה בעת קשה כזאת להלחם באיזה דבר שאיננו מהמחוייב בארח ישר למטרתכם אין זה אלא קלות הדעת ומיעוט תשומת לב לתפקידכם .

Therefore, if you are fighting religion and nationalism because they directly hinder your goal, this is reasonable and acceptable. However, if you are fighting religion and nationalism when they do no direct harm to your goal, this is a crime and evil-mindedness. It is like a poor man who hardly earns enough money for bread and water, but spoils all his earnings by buying wine and drinks, and by doing so, fades away and dies.

Is it not enough for you, in your difficult war—which is your main focus and is entirely against the nature of man—when you are part of the masses to work and toil without any motivation? And is this war not enough that you add fuel to the flame by also fighting at the same time against religion and nationalism? Is there a greater foolishness in the world than this? The main thing is that you will perish very quickly, and therefore, you are stepping backwards and your work is bearing curse.

The truth is that until now you had no other choice because these two ways present the most terrible opposition to your method, according to their nature that they have received from the bourgeois middle class.

But in the manner that I have laid my method before you, religion not only does not oppose and damage you, but it is the most effective assistant, and it is also the only instrument that ensures the success of your goal in the most uplifting manner.

As for nationalism, my opinion is that it's better if it were to be corrected. It should be given a proper character—one that will be accepted by the masses—before it is completely uprooted and fought against.

Surely the most I can do is to present you with a successful mechanism to obtain the goal; but the work and trouble themselves are all upon you to find a suitable plan and to supply it with swift and loyal legs to spread the word quickly. If this is acceptable to you, let me know or send me suitable people. Then we can work out a successful plan to ensure swift expansion.

לכן אם אתם לוחמים על הדת והנאציונליזם בשביל שהוא מזיק בארח ישר למטרתכם הוא סבור ומקובל אולם אם אתם לוחמים על הדת והנאציונליזם בשעה שאינו מזיק למטרתכם הרי זה פשע וזדון לב בדומה לעני שמרויח על לחם צר ומים לחץ בדוחק והוא משחית רוחיו על יינות ומשקאות וע׳כ (ועל כן) הולך ונאבד ונגווע.

כי המצער לכם מלחמתכם הקשה שהוא לעיקר הגדול שלכם הנמצא כולו כנגד טבעו של אדם בהיותכם מצוים להמונים לעבוד ולהתייגע בלי שום מאטיוו פאוור ומעט לכם מלחמה זו, אתם מוסיפים אש על המדורה להלחם באותו העת גם עם הדת ועם הנאציונליזם היש בעולם קלות הדעת יותר מזה והעיקר הוא כי אבוד תאבודו מהרה וע׳כ ועל כן אתם הולכים אחורנית והקללה מצוייה בעבדתכם.

הן אמת אשר עד עתה לא הי׳ להם לכם עצה אחרת בהיות שני הדרכים האלו מתנגדים היותר נוראים לשיטתכם ע׳פ על פי האופי שלהם שקבלו מאת הבורגנים .

אולם כפי אשר ערכתי לכם את שיטתי הנה הדת לא מלבד שאינו מתנגד ומזיק לכם רק הוא המסייע היותר מוצלח והוא לבד המכשיר הבטוח להצלחת מטרתכם במדה היותר נעלה.

ובדבר הנאציונליזם דעתי היא שצריך ומוטב לתקנו וליתן לו אופי מותאם שיקובל על לב המונים בטרם לעקרו לגמרי ולהלחם עמו.

אמנם כמובן שלכל היותר אין ביכלתי יותר רק מלהמציא לכם המכונה המוצלחה למטרתה אמנם הטרחה והעבודה עצמה מוטל כולה עליכם להמציא תכנית מותאמה וליתן לה רגלים זריזים ונאמנים להתפשטות המהירה ואם דבר זה מקובל עליכם הרי לכם להודיעני או לשלוח אלי אנשים המתאימים ואז נעבד תכנית מוצלחה באופן התפשטותה המהירה.

Chapter Four:
The Successful Way

Advice on how to progress:

There is nothing that we can grasp intellectually today that has not already been explained by the generations before us because inheritance in intellectual matters is similar to inheritance in material possessions. We do not possess anything material other than what has been left to us by our forefathers from generation to generation. Only according to the degree of the inheritance are we able to add some known fixed percentage. In exactly the same manner, the intellectual possessions that our forefathers amassed throughout the generations, even if not published in books, are still not lost but are universally available in the atmosphere of the world.

So that anyone who starts dealing with these intellectual issues draws immediately all the questions and answers that previous generations had discovered relevant to that issue. Hence, it becomes much easier for him to inquire on the issue and to understand it. Therefore, when we deal with an issue that our fathers have not inquired into all the way to the end, we are not able to sufficiently understand it and to make it completely clear. We can only add some part to it as we are groping in the dark, and the matter remains in this state for the generations after us until the Creator adds it to an appropriate critical mass and the last generation completes it.

פרק רביעי:
דרך המוצלח

עצה להתקדמות:

אין תפיסא לנו בהשכליים אשר עדיין לא נתבררו בדורות שלפנינו כי הירושה בשכלים דומה לירושה בקנינים הגשמים וכמו שאין לנו בגשמיות רק מה שהשאירו לנו אבותינו מדור דור שלפי שיעור הירושה אנו מסוגלים להוסיף אחוזים ידועים קבועים עד'ז על דרך זה ממש גם קנינים השכליים אשר רכשו אבותינו מדור דור אע'פ אף על פי שלא נדפסו בספרים מ'מ מכל מקום אינם נאבדים רק נשארים צרורים באויר העולם

באופן שכל מי שמתחיל למשמש באותם המושכלות תיכף נמשכים אליו כל השאלות ותשובות שדורות שלפניו גילו באותו המושכל וע'כ ועל כן בנקל לו מאד לעמוד על המושכל ולבררו לכן אם אנו עוסקים באיזה מושכל אשר אבותינו לא עסקו בו כל צרכו אין גם אנו יכולים לעמוד עליו ולבררו לגמרי אלא להוסיף איזה שיעור בעלטה ונשאר העיניין לדורות אחרינו עד שיצרפו השי'ת לשיעור הגון ודור האחרון ישלים אותו.

Inheriting intellectual issues:

Therefore you can see that, for example, in psychology, we do not succeed as in other branches of knowledge, while on the other hand, in mathematics, we succeed more than in any other field. This is not because one is hard and the other is easy, but rather because of what we have inherited. Our fathers dealt extensively with mathematics and have left us a large inheritance, while psychologists have not left us anything important, and therefore it is difficult for us to inquire and find out; we can only take things further on and leave them for future generations.

Why there is no progress in Divinity:

Out of this [discussion], a major question emerges. We find that when it comes to Divine wisdom, our fathers dealt with this more than with any other field of knowledge. So how is it that we are still poorer in this knowledge more than any other knowledge in the world?

One cannot separate the mind and the body. One should know that it is a rule in all [aspects of] knowledge that it cannot be revealed to us in all its purity unless this does us some good. If it does us any harm, than we can be sure that the knowledge will become completely vague. And even if someone, will push it and force it into our brains, it will not stay there long—we will scatter it away and forget all about it.

Blurring of the mind of truth:

It is known that there is no righteous person in this world who has never sinned. Therefore, when we come to dealing with Divine lessons, we are immediately filled with the fear of punishment, if this is confirmed as true. This means that knowledge becomes a source of sorrow for them, and in this case, the knowledge will, as a must, immediately blur out. Or even when it is explained to him by

ירושת המושכלות:

ולפיכך תראה אשר למשל בפסיכו-לוגיא אין אנו מצליחים כמו בשאר חכמות והיפוכו בחכמת החשבון אנו מצליחים יותר מבשאר החכמות אין זאת מטעם קל וקשה אלא מטעם הירושה כי אבותינו עסקו הרבה בחשבון והשאירו לנו ירושה גדולה והפסיכולוגיא לא השאירו לנו דבר חשוב וע׳כ ועל כן קשה לנו לברר רק להמשיך דברים ולהשאירם לדורות אחרינו.

למה אין התקדמות באלקיות:

ומזה יצא לנו שאלה גדולה הלא אנו מוצאים אשר בחכמת אלקיות עסקו בהם אבותינו במדה מרובה על כל שאר החכמות וא׳כ על מה אנו דלים בחכמה הזאת עוד יותר מכל המושכלות שבעול

אין להפריד שכל מהגוף אמנם תדע שחוק הוא בכל מושכ׳ מושכלות שלא יוכל להתגלות לנו בטהרו אם הוא אינו מסבב לנו שום טובה ואם מסבב לנו עוד רעה הרי יכולים אנו להיות בטוחים שהמושכל יתטשטש לגמרי ואפילו אם אחד ידחוק אותו בהכרח וכפיה לתוך מוחותינו לא ישהא שמה זמן מרובה אלא נפריחנו ונשכיחהו.

טשטוש שכל האמת:

ונודע שאין צדיק בארץ אשר לא יחטא וע׳כ ועל כן כשבאים לעסוק במושכלות אלקיות תיכף יפול עליהם פחד העונשים אם יתאמת להם ונמצא המושכל גורם להם צער אשר במצב כזה מוכרח תיכף המושכל להטשטש או אפי׳ אפילו בהתברר לו ע׳ על ידי אחר מוכרח

another, then immediately it has to be totally forgotten. This "newborn" cannot live on because the body has no satisfaction from it and would not want to sustain it and allow it to exist.

The denial:

And therefore, we find a great denial of existence of Providence even though it definitely applies within the reality and existence of the [four domains]: the Inanimate, the Vegetative, the Animal, and the Speaking [human]. [Those who deny] develop in their imagination a blind Supervisor, whom they call Nature, which even common sense cannot accept, since there cannot be a more blurred theory than this. But nevertheless, many nearly everyone—believe in it. And all this is because the knowledge, if indeed confirmed as valid, would be the source of great sorrow for them because of their sin and iniquity.

And therefore, any scholar, who is anxious for the Word of the Creator, is obliged to completely remove from his mind the matter of future reward and punishment because ultimately this is incomprehensible and is beyond the grasp of the human mind. Surely [reward and punishment] is not about revenge and bearing grudges, but more like washing out the filth that the soul has taken upon itself. This being the case, why would one call it punishment? On the contrary, it would only be wishful thinking that the Merciful One would send His greatest wrath upon him and redeem him! Indeed, every person finds this difficult to accept with his common sense while he does not feel the Divine delight, he thinks, "I'd rather experience neither His joys nor His wrath (lit. neither the honey nor the sting)." This way of thinking is considered a great misfortune.

There are also punishments that are extended from sins by means of cause and effect. Even these should not cause any fear because of the earlier mentioned reasoning, because when we approach the Divine study, we have already gotten rid of our iniquities and have received our punishment. If this were not so, we would not be at all ready

תיכף להיות שכוח מעקרו ואין הולד הזה בן קיימא כי הגוף אין לו נחת ממנו ולא ירצה לפרנסו ולקיימו.

ההכחשה:

ולפיכך אנו מוצאים כפירה גדולה במציאות השגחה וע״פ ועל פי שנוהגת בהכרח במציאות והתקימות הדצח״ם דומם, צומח, חי, מדבר ומדמים לעצמם משגיח עור טבע יכנהו הגם שאין הדעת סובלו שאין לך סברא מטושטשת יותר מזה עכ״ז עם כל זה יחזיקו בה רבים וכמעט כולם וכל זה הוא מפני שהמושכל אם יתאמת להם יסבב להם צער גדול מחמת חטאם ועוונם.

ולפיכך כל משכיל וחרד על דבר ה׳ מחוייב להעתיק לגמרי משכלו ענין השו״ע השכר ועונש העתידי כי סוף סוף אינו מובן ונתפס כלל לשכל האנושי שהרי בלי ספק אינם נקימות ונטורות אלא בח״י בחינת כבוס מהזוהמה שלקחה עליה הנשמה ואם כן איך יכונה זה לעונש אדרבא כל כי האי רתחא ירתח רחמנא עלן ויגאלנו אכן אין אדם יכול לקבל את זה בשכלו הפשוט בשעה שאינו מרגיש את נועם אלוקי הוא חושב לא מדובשו ולא מעוקצו ולפיכך לרעה גדולה יחשב אלה בתפיסתו.

גם שיש עונשים נמשכים מחטאים בדרך קודם ונמשך וגם מאלה אין לפחוד מטעם הנ״ל כי בו בשעה שאנו מתקרבים להעיון האלקי כבר נפטרנו מעוונותינו וקבלנו עונשינו דאי לאו הכי שאם לא כן לא היינו מוכנים כלל לעיון הקדוש הזה וממ״נ ממה נפשך אם מתאמת

for this Holy learning; and in any case, if [such learning] becomes true for [a person], then he is [already] Cleaved to [the Creator], and certainly he will be blessed and have had already received his punishment. And if it does not become true, then he is not in a state of Cleaving and has no reason to be afraid of the punishment.

The Work:

In order to merit the truth, Work is surely needed, for the little one has actions but no thoughts. Rather, his thought derives from his actions, and if he is not afraid of punishment, he could start spiritually working with the One Precept, which is: Loving the Creator and loving His created beings as mentioned in the article *Love your neighbor as yourself* [in the book *Wisdom of Truth*]. And if one is doing a lot of Work, he should be happy because he brought near the time of his redemption. And if he does little [Work], he should hope for the help of the Creator or pray. Yet, one cannot know and he should not wonder about the past, because loving other created beings is something that all mankind accept.

Ninety-nine percent is Loving Others:

You should know that there is nothing more blurring for one's mind than wondering about the *Rishonot* (words of the first sages)—because it immediately creates for him a firm wall so as to not let true mind, not even a speck truth, into his heart—so that his mind will not mislead him to take on more bother. Therefore, if he is Working only in the aspect of the Love-thy-Neighbor mode, that is, actually in the ninety-nine percent—with the only condition being that by doing so he will merit the purification of his body and Cleaving to the Creator—then he will not wonder, no matter what, about the *Rishonot* (words of the first sages) because that [type of] Work is already accepted by all humankind. And due to the final goal, there is no additional bother and it is not possible to regret it.

לו הרי הוא דבוק בו ית' ובודאי הוא ברוך וקיבל מכבר עונשו ואם משלם אינו מתאמת לו הלא אינו דבוק ולמה יפחד מעונש.

העבודה:

וכדי לזכות לאמת צריכים ודאי עבודה כי הקטן יש לו מעשה ואין לו מחשבה אלא מחשבתו נמשכת מתוך מעשיו - ואם אינו מפחד מעונשים יוכל להתחיל בעבודה במצווה אחת שהיא אהבתו ית' ואהבת בריותיו כמ"ש כמו שכתוב בקונטרס ואהבת לרעך כמוך ואם מרבה בעבודה ישמח כי קירב גאולתו ואם ממעט יקווה לה' או יתפלל אלא אומנם אין לדעת משום זה ואין לתהות על ראשונות כי אהבת הבריות דבר מקובל לכל אדם.

צ'ט 99 אחוזי ם בא"ז באהבת זולתו:

ודע שאין לך מטשטש שכלו ביותר מן האדם התוהא על ראשונות - כי תיכף עושה לו חומה בצורה שלא לעזוב שכל אמת ואפי ואפילו ספק אמת לתוך לבו - כדי שלא יטעהו שכלו להוסיף בטרחות ולפיכך אם הוא עובד רק בבח' בבחינת אהבת זולתו דהיינו בתשעים ותשעה אחוז ממש רק בתנאי שמתוך כך יזכה לצירוף הגוף ולדביקות השי"ת אז לא יהיה עכ"פ על כל פנים תוהא על ראשונות כי העבודה הזאת מקובלת בלאו הכי על כל אדם ומטעם המטרה הסופית אין בזה שום טרחה נוספת ולא יתכן להתחרט עליו.

The need for a Rav (spiritual teacher):

With all this, surely one would need a truly learned Rav because it is not possible to accept things deep in the heart from dead sages but rather only from living ones. This is naturally so, and how much more so in such an important matter as this. And all that has been said above is based on the point discussed earlier, namely that the main thing is the purification of the body so that it is able to share. And with this, loving one's neighbor is more useful than the work between mankind and the Creator (see the article: "Giving of the Torah on Mount Sinai" and "Mutual Responsibility" in the book *Wisdom of Truth*). But he needs to work a lot and also have determination and strong acceptance in order for him not to do anything for his own sake. And in this way, he will merit complete faith and will also be able to fulfill the Torah and the Precepts wholeheartedly and with a glad heart. And the neglect, during the period of his training, would not damage him at all. And this is what is referred to in the saying: "Out of studying the Torah Not For Its Own Sake, the studying For Its Own Sake emerges." And also it is written: "Charity saves from death." (Proverbs 10:2) And also what Hillel the Elder said: "Love your neighbor as yourself."

הצורך לרב:

ועם כל אלה ודאי לרב משכיל אמיתי הוא צריך כי אי אפשר לקבל דברים על הלב מחכמים המתים זולת מהחיים דוקא כי כן הוא הטבע ואצ"ל ואין צורך לומר בעינין חמור כזה. וכל הנ"ל נסמך על עניין המדובר שהעיקר הוא צירוף הגוף שיהא מסוגל להשפיע ובזה אהבת זולתו יותר מועיל מהעבודות שבין אדם למקום (עיין קונטרס מתן תורה וערבות) אלא לריבוי עבודה הוא צריך ולהחלטה והסכמה חזקה שלא יעשה כלום לצורך עצמו שבדרך זה יזכה לאמונה שלימה ולקיום תורה ומצוות בלב שלם ושמח ולא יזיק לו כלום ההזנחה בעת הכשרתו ועל כגון זה אמרו מתוך שלא לשמה יבוא לשמה וכן צדקה תציל מוות וכן מאמר הלל הנשיא ואהבת לרעך כמוך.

Chapter Five: Altruism that Depends on Excessive Egoism

The existence of various spiritual forms:

We should not revoke any form of spirituality from among those who have gained for themselves a right to exist in some corner of the globe. Even if they oppose more important forms, still they should not be revoked and eradicated (lit. murdered). However, boundaries should be set between them, with more given to the more important forms and less to the less important forms. This division should occur in each and every country, but it should not be done in smaller collectives because then the method would be damaged. Here is the rule: If we understand the prohibition against the killing of people, even if they are of the lowest class and the least intelligence, then, needless to say, how much more severe is it in the case of spiritual forms and ideas, whether good or spoiled, that have taken hold somewhere in the world—because everything has its own space.

Leaving the boundaries:

This is yet another reason to leave the boundaries between countries as they are because every country has its own ideas and ancestral heritage, some important and some less important, and the prohibition against murder applies to all of them.

Idol worshipping cannot be revoked unless done by its practitioners:

Surely it is not our duty to coerce people who support a certain lower level idea if they have started using it. On the contrary, when an idea is being discarded by its believers, this indicates that it [the idea] no longer brings any benefit, because every idea needs time

פרק חמישי:
אלטרואיזם התלוי בעגאיזם המופרז

קיום כל מיני צורות רוחניות:

אסור לנו לבטל שום צורה מצורת הרוחניות אשר רכשה לה באיזה פינה בעולם זכות קיום ואע"פ ואף על פי שהמה מתנגדים לצורות יותר חשובות עכ"ז עם כל זה אסור לבטלה ולרצחה נפש אמנם יש להטיל גבולים ביניהם אשר הריבוי ינתן לצורות היותר חשובות והמיעוט לצורות הפחותות וחלוקה זו צריכה להיות בכל מדינה ומדינה ואסור להרשות זה לקיבוצים קטנים פן יקלקלו את השיטה - וזה הכלל אם מובן לנו איסור רציחה בגופים ואפילו בפחותי עם ושוטים אצ'ל אין צורך לומר שחמורה היא בצורות רוחניות ואידיאות שקנו להם מקום בעולם אם טובים אם קלים - כי אין לך דבר שאין לו מקום.

השארת תחומין:

וזהו טעם נוסף להשארת תחומין בין האומות שכל אומה יש לה אידאות ומורשת אבות משלה הן חשובין והן פחותין ואיסור רציחה שוה בכלם

אין ע"ז (עבודה זרה) נבטלת אלא בעובדיה:

אמנם ודאי שאין לנו חוב לכוף אנשים שיהיו נושאים לאיזו אידיאה פחותה אם התחילו לשמש עמה כי אדרבה כל אידיאה אשר עובדיה משליכים אותה סימן הוא שכבר אבדה כל תועלתה - כי

for development and growth until one can grasp whether the idea is good or whether it is bad. And this is the entire vitality of the lesser ideas that we have to deal with. That is, we have to see their inferiority because understanding evil has as much value in the process of gaining wisdom as understanding good.

"However much you enjoy, to that extent you are taking away from My world; and however much you cause others to enjoy, to that extent you are causing delight to Me and I will be proud of you. And to the extent that I am proud of you, I will bestow on you glory and wisdom and pleasure and delight, with full generosity. And if you enjoy, you will cause lack in My world, and then My ire shall be raised against you, and this lack will be your responsibility. Woe to those who are partying in My vineyard! Each one digging with a hoe, as a miner in his mine, then hides the bounty in their bag and runs away."

Family egoism and individual egoism:

Excessive egoism was given to people only to develop love. It is as if someone wants to plant a fruit tree. To do that, he has to first find the seed that pertains to that tree, and afterwards, through work and development, you will finally merit seeing its fruit. And so with cultivating love: You have to start with a nucleus that is capable of giving rise to [love]. And I shall tell you this: [This nucleus] is the individual egoism, with all its disadvantages, dwelling as it is on jealousy and lust and pride. Then, through family life, the narrow egoism develops and extends to include the whole family because the person loves his spouse as his own self and his children as his own self. And thus narrow egoism is extended into a wider territory, and this is what has been prepared by the **first level** of nature, namely the animal instinct within all of us. And afterwards, a quality was found in human beings, to be in need of a life of togetherness with others, and thereby his egoism widens to include the entire neighborhood, or the city, or the country, because a person's own individual good depends, to a great extent, on the entirety of this community. And this is the **second level**, which is natural as well.

לכל אידיאה צריכין זמן פיתוח וגידול עד שמרגישים אם טובה היא אם רעה היא וזהו כל החיות שבאידיאות הפחותות אשר יש לנו בטיפולם דהיינו לראות את פחיתותם כי הבנת הרע היא חשובה בערכי החכמה כמו הבנת הטוב.

כמה שאתה נהנה כאותו השיעור אתה מחסר בעולמי וכמה שאתה מהנה לזולתך כשיעורו אתה מהנה אותי ואתפאר בך וכפי השיעור שאהנה ממך אעשה לך תפארה וחכמה נועם ועונג כידי הטובה ואם תהנה תחסר שיעור הנאתך בעולמי ואז יחרה אפי בך והחסרון הזה על ראשך יחול. הוי ההוללים בכרמי כל איש במעדר יעדור כחוצב במחצבת ויטמון בכליו ויברח

עגאיזם המשפחתי ועגאיזם הפרטי:

לא ניתן העגאיזם המופרז אל הבריות רק להתפתחות האהבה: ודומה הדבר כמו שנרצה לנטוע אילן מאכל הרי אתה מוכרח מתחילה למצוא הגרעין המיוחס להאילן הזה ואח'כ ואחר כך ע"י על ידי עבודה והתפתחות תיזכה לראות פריו כן לצמיחת האהבה צרכין עכ'פ על כל פנים גרעין מסוגל אליה ואומר לך שהוא העגאיזם הפרטי עם כל החסרונות שבו המתגלגלין על גלגל הקנאה ותאוה וכבוד אח'כ אחר כך ע"י על ידי חיי משפחה מתפתח העגואיזם הצר ומתרחב על כל המשפחה כי אוהב את אשתו כמותו ואח"כ ואחר כך את בניו כמותו ונמצא עגואיזם הצר נתרחב על שטח רחב וזהו שהוכשר בטבע הא' כלומר הבהמי המשותף ואח'כ ואחר כך נמצא סגולה במין האדם להזדקק לחיי חיבור ואז מתרחב לו העגואיזם להקיף את כל שטח שכניו העיר או המדינה בהיות שטובתו הפרטית תלוי במידה מרובה בכל הציבור הזה וזהו דרגה ב' שגם הוא טבעי.

Then the work starts to become more profound: to understand that the foreigners who have only recently come to settle in his community also must be given as much love as the people of his own town. [These foreigners] may be poor at the moment, but following the path of "the wise maintains his foresight" (lit. the wise has his eyes in his head), he can foresee that with time, it is possible for them to become rich and he would enjoy their company.

The degree of love:

And the path of education brings people a lot closer. This means understanding the degree in its entirety, which is "Love your friend as yourself." (Leviticus 19:18) [Understanding it] starts with what is said: "Do not ignore your own flesh," (Isaiah 58:7) that means, [loving] members of your family; for this, it is not necessary to demonstrate it to a specific degree. When it comes to life of community, it is necessary to demonstrate the degree of "Love your friend as yourself." And also, in regards to the foreigner, too "love him as yourself."

A good order of development for love:

At first, one should become strong in loving oneself to the fullest degree because the nature of a human being from infancy is to be lazy. And even when it comes to our own good we are comfortable to neglect the work; this is why there is jealousy, lust, pride...."

Altruism depends on egoism:

After this, it is necessary to climb up the above-mentioned stages to the same degree that one has already attained and earned for oneself, as it is said: "Love your friend as yourself." And regarding the foreigners, it is said: "...and you shall love him as yourself." (Leviticus 19:34) This means that from the start, a person must work to love himself as a person also causes and awakens his self-love each and every day because of his laziness and irresponsibility. It is only

אח'ז אחרי זה מתחיל העבודה להתחזק להבין אשר גם הגרים הבאים רק עתה להיתישב בשכונתו צריך להשרות עלהים האהבה כמו על בני עירו הגם שעתה עניים הם אולם בדרך החכם עיניו בראשו אפשר להשכיל שבדרך הזמן יכולין להתעשר ויהנה מקרבתם.

שיעור האהבה:

וסדר החינוך מקרב הרבה דהיינו להבין השיעור בשלימותו שהוא ואהבת לרעך כמוך שמתחילה נאמר ומבשרך אל תתעלם דהיינו רק בני משפחתו וע'ז ועל זה אינם צריכין להראות שיעור אמנם על חיי הצבור צריכין להראות השיעור ואהבת לרעך כמוך וכן על הגר ואהבת לו כמוך

סדר התפתחות טובה לאהבה:

שמתחלה צריך להתחזק באהבת עצמו בשיעור מלא כי טבע האדם מנעוריו להיות עצל, אפילו במה שמגיע לטובתו עצמו לעבדא בהפקירא ניחא ליה כי נוח לו להפקיר את העבודה וע'ז ועל זה היכי קנאה, תאוה, כבוד.

אלטרואיזם תלוי בעגעיזם:

אח"ז אחרי זה צריכין לילך במדרגות הנ'ל באותו השיעור שכבר השיג והרויח לעצמו כמ'ש כמו שכתוב: ואהבת לרעך כמוך ועל הגר כתוב ואהבת לו כמוך (קדושים, יט:לד) ואין הכונה אלא רק שצריך מתחילה לעבוד שיאהב את עצמו כי גם האדם מועל ומאנה את אהבת עצמו בכל יום מטעם העצלות והפקרות. ואחר שקונה

after he acquires the narrow egoism, namely, the excessive self-love, then he can extend that love to include others in it. With this you can understand that…

…true altruism depends on excessive egoism:

Anyone who has not attained love of himself—in the full sense of the word, but rather is a person of no consequence or a person of no importance, does not even have the seed of love. And whoever extends his own love of self, and then, through education, extends it to love others. Such a person is the real great and true person.

The mistake in abandoning nationalism:

Here we can see the great mistake in principle in abandoning nationalism because successful internationalism completely depends on successful nationalism, as mentioned earlier. Because everything is necessary, nothing is harmful, except that we need proper regulations and education.

Loathed means harmful:

One should remember the rule that nothing is loathsome and contemptuous, save only in our interpretation of the degree of its harm and benefit, its beauty and praiseworthiness. For example, it is not fit to protect a garden to have beauty and splendor if it is not useful for its growth. On the other hand, garbage and dirt are beneficial for the garden because they are useful to it and help it grow. So if we detest our egoism, it should be to the degree that it causes damage to the people in the world. But once we know the craft of utilizing our narrow egoism for the good of the community, [then] surely it [should be] considered beautiful and worthy of praise.

העגאיזם הצר דהיינו אהבת עצמו המופרז אז אפשר לו להרחיב האהבה על זולתו ובזה תבין ש...

... אלטרואיזם אמיתי תלוי בעגאיזם מופרז:

כי מי שלא השיג אהבת עצמו במלא מובן המילה אלא הוא בבח׳ בבחינת הפקר או אדם של מה בכך ודאי שאין לו אפ׳ אפילו הגרעין של אהבה ומי שהולך ומרחיב את אהבת עצמו ואח׳כ ואחר כך ע׳י על ידי חינוך הולך ומעבירו על אהבת זולתו הוא האדם הגדול האמיתי.

הטעות לבטל הנציואנאליזם:

ובזה תראה הטעות הגדול לבטל את הנציונליזם מעקרו כי האינטרנאציליזם המוצלח תלוי לגמרי בנאציליזם המוצלח כנ׳ל אלא הכל צריך ואין כאן דבר מזיק ורק לסדרים ולחינוך אנו צרכין.

מאוס פירושו מזיק:

צריך לזכור הכלל הזה שאין דבר מאוס ומזולזל רק בפירושם בשיעור הזיקם והמועיל בו היופי וכל שבח למשל שאין נאה ומשובח לשמור על הגן מיופי והידור שאינו מועיל לצמיחה ואדרבה כל זבל ולכלוך משובח ונאה לגן באשר שמועילו ומצמיחו ואם אנו מואסים בעגאיזם הוא בשיעור שהוא מזיק לישוב העולם אמנם בהודיע לנו אותו המלאכה איך לנצל את העגואיזם הצר בשביל טובת הישוב הנה ודאי לשבח ויופי יחשב.

The development and progress depends on providence over those who fail:

This is because whoever excels in collecting all the profits, small and large, and whoever is able to reach the desired benefit is the one who is in haste to secure the desired goal. And whoever is lazy or does not pay attention to utilizing everything that can be utilized for the sake of that which is useful is the one who pushes away the goal and also does damage. From this, an absolute law emerges, which is: Whoever wants to succeed in his or her business should not miss anything, not even a small item, that is fit to be utilized for the purpose of his or her business.

You cannot trust the mind:

This is because the mind does not govern the body, and a person has neither faith nor trust except to preserve himself and his offspring when they need him, being that this is how things are prepared by nature. This is a dominating physical force.

Trust by acquisition:

Indeed, there is still a way for the proper trust to gain a foothold in a person through acquisition, and it is trust in the Creator. Trust in one's friend, even though he has gained trust, it is still not true trust because it must be conditional (lit. depends on something). Since nothing can be eternal, then this trust cannot be eternal and therefore, there is no trust here. This is not the case with regards to the Creator. Although [trust] is conditional nevertheless it fits to be eternal since the Creator is eternal. For this reason, they have said: "From Not For Its Own Sake, he shall come to For Its Own Sake."

ההתפתחות והקדימה הוא כפי ההשגחה בניכשלים:

כי כל המרבה לאסוף כל הרוחים הקטנים עם הגדולים וכל המסוגל לתועלת הרצוי הריהו ממהר ומבטיח את התכלית המקווה וכל המתעצל או אינו נותן לב לנצל כל דבר שראוי לנצלו לטובת המועיל הריהו מרחיק את התכלית וגם מזיקו ומזה יוצא לנו חוק מוחלט שהרוצה הצלחה בעסקו אל יחמיץ אפ׳ אפילו דבר קטן הראוי לנצלו לתועלת עסקו.

אין נאמנות בשכל:

משום שהשכל אינו שולט בגוף ואין לאדם אמונה ונאמנות זולת על "שמירת עצמו" ועל יוצאי יריכו בזמן שצריכים אליו לטעם היותם מוכנים כן בטבע והיא כח גופני בעל השליטה.

אמונה בקנין:

ויש אמנם עוד מקום אמונה הראויה לשכון באדם בדרך קנין והוא האמונה בהשי״ת אמנם בחבירו אע״פ אף על פי שקנה בו האמונה מ״מ מכל מקום אינו נאמנות משום היותה בהכרח תלויה בדבר ואין לך דבר שיה׳ נצחי וממילא שגם האמונה אינו נצחי וע״כ ועל כן אין כאן נאמנות משא״כ מה שאין כן בהשי״ת הגם שתלוי בדבר מ״מ מכל מקום ראוי הדבר להיות נצחי כמו שהשי״ת הוא נצחי וע״ז ועל זה אמרו מתוך שלא לשמה בא לשמה.

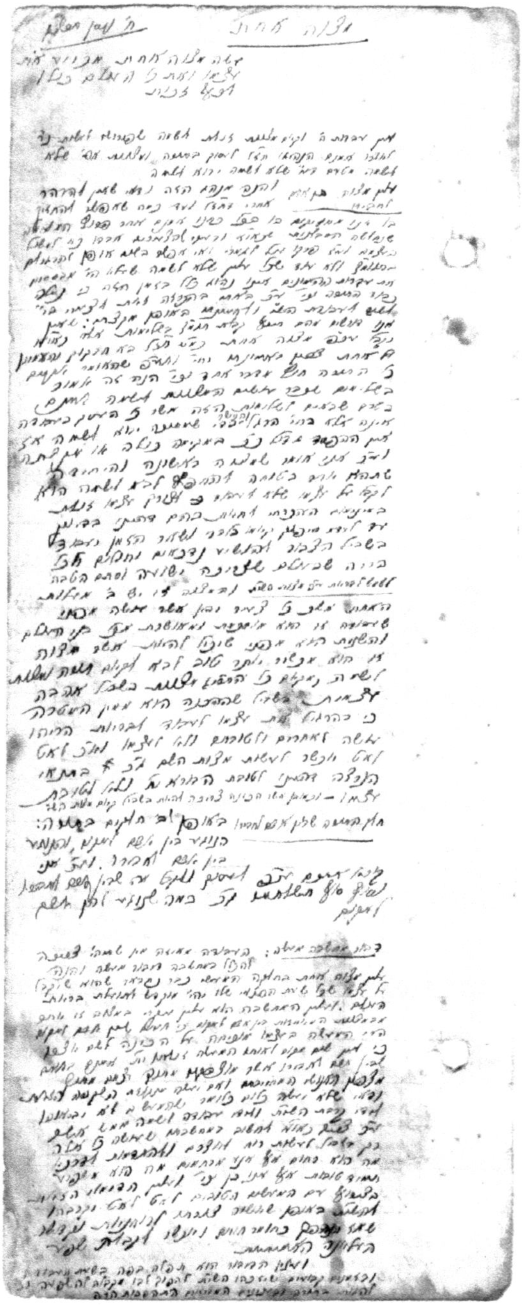
ה' עמן חשון
מצוה אחת

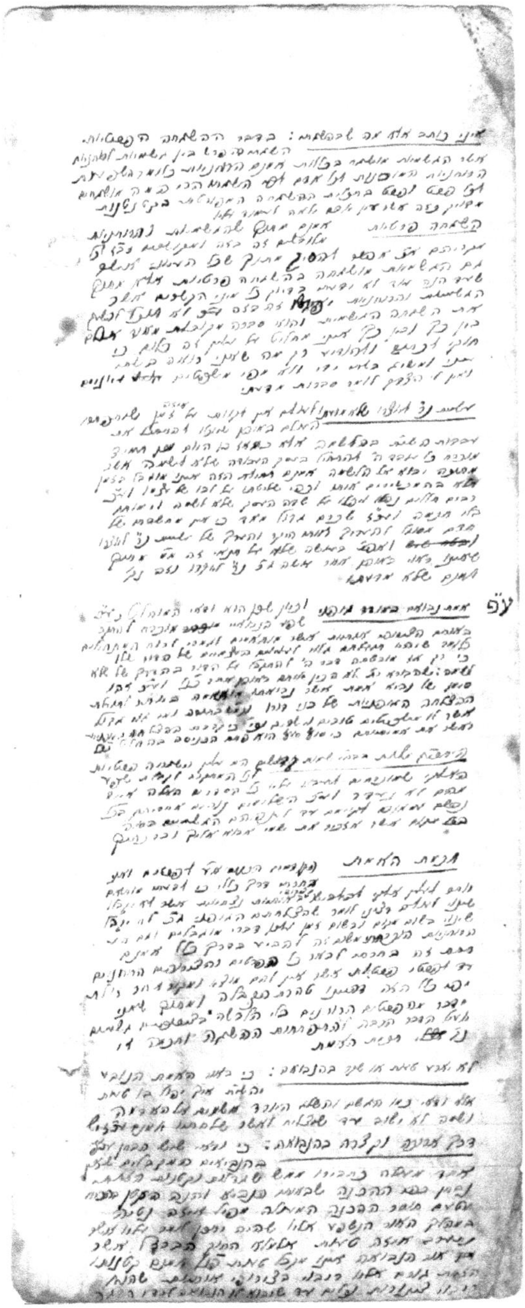

Original Handwritten Article of One Precept

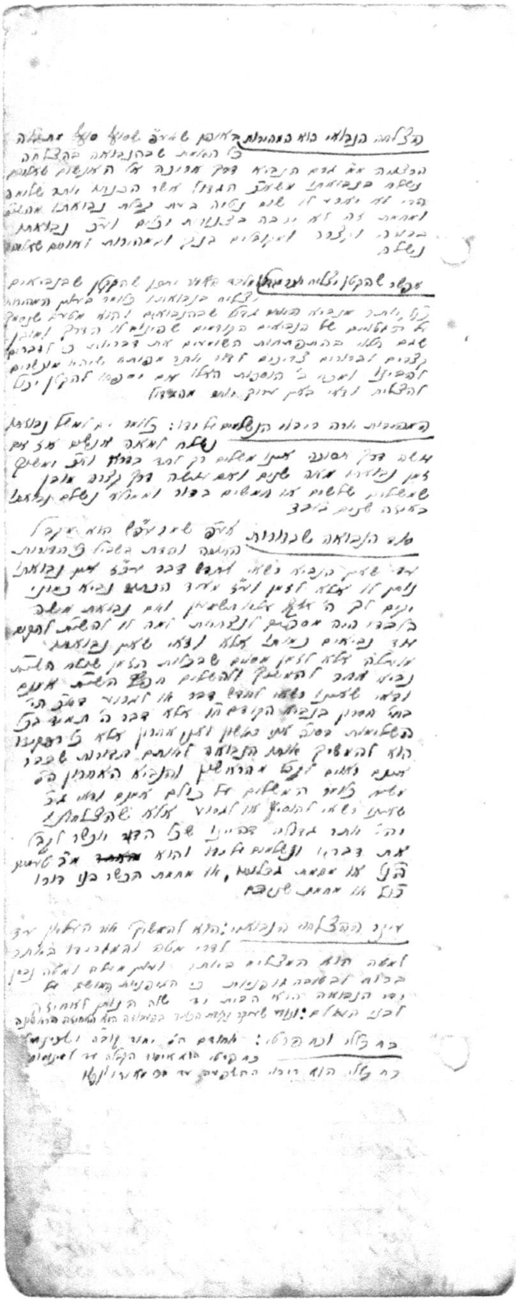

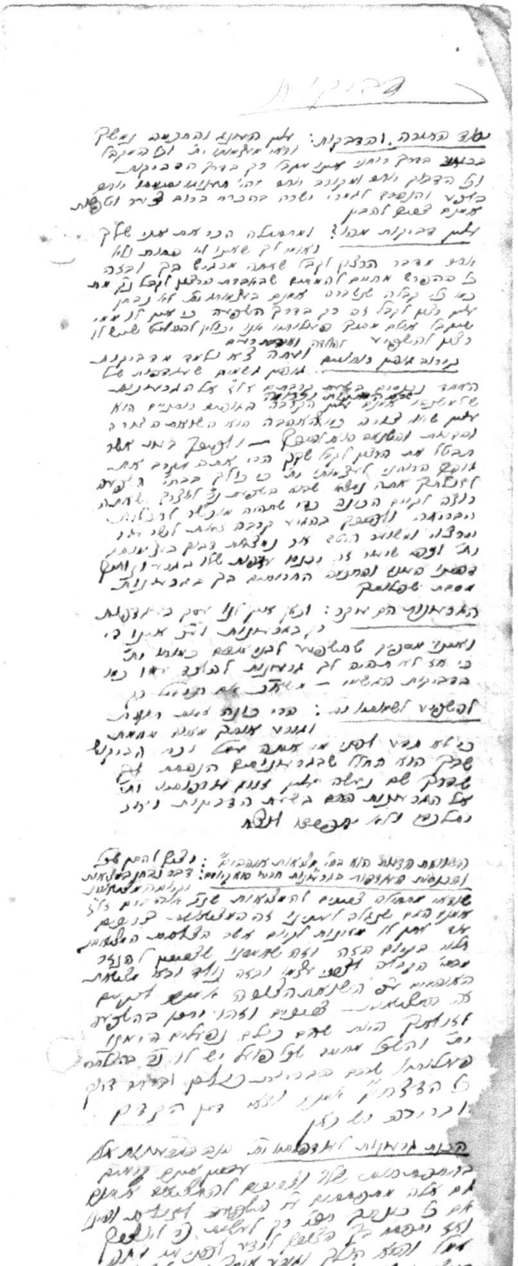

Original Handwritten Article of One Precept

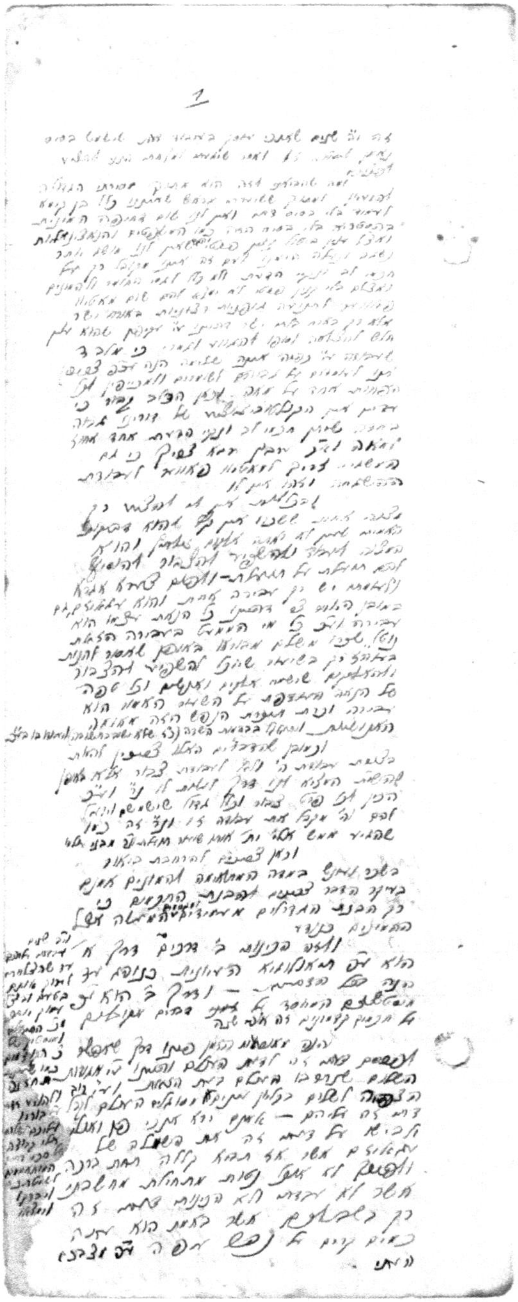

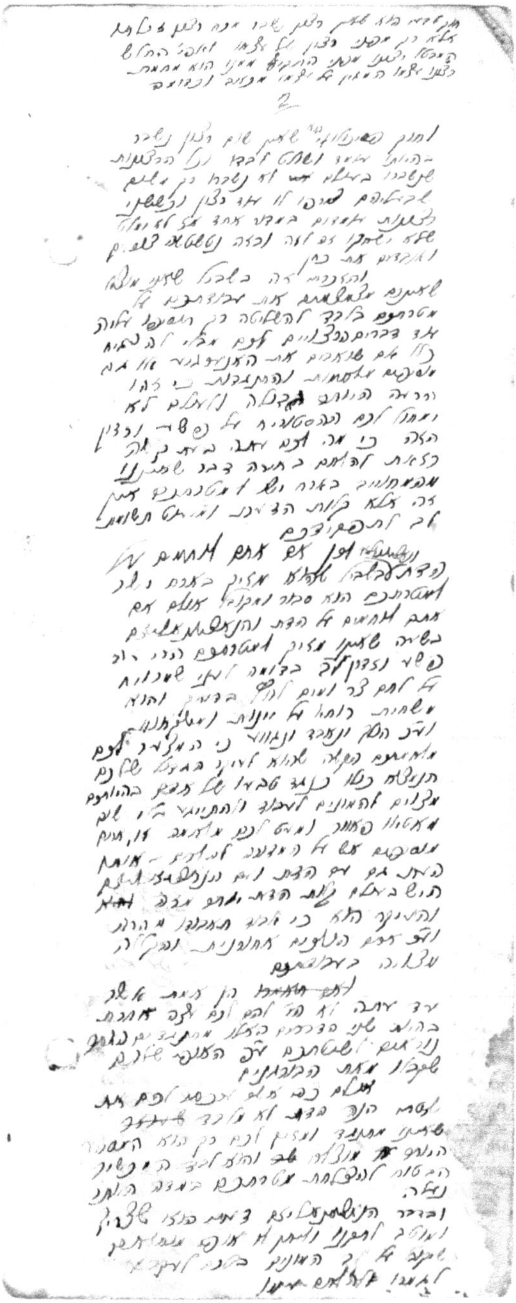

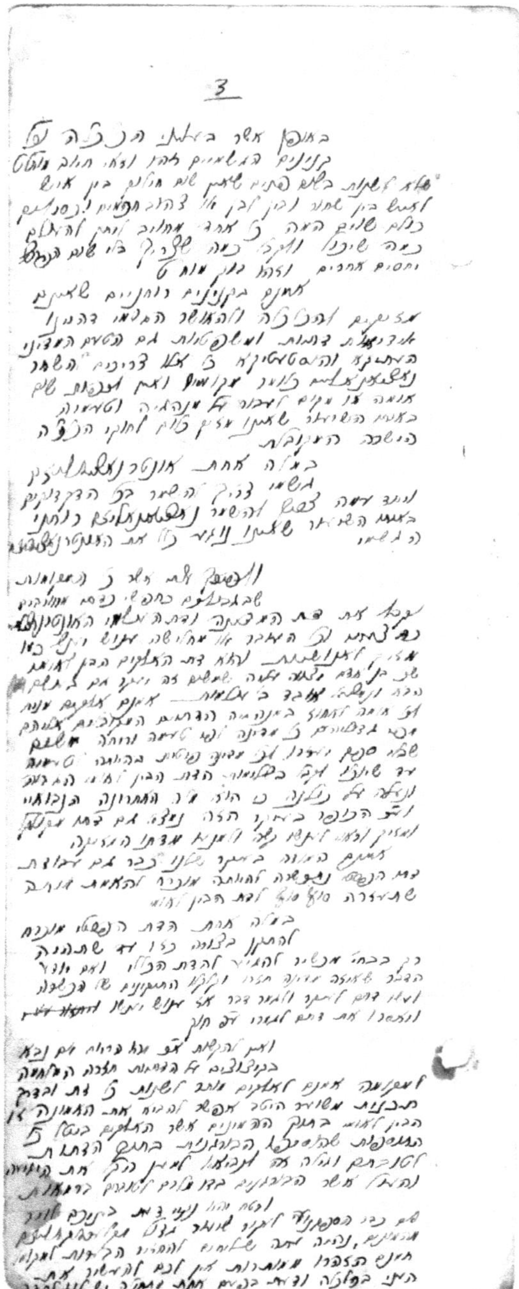

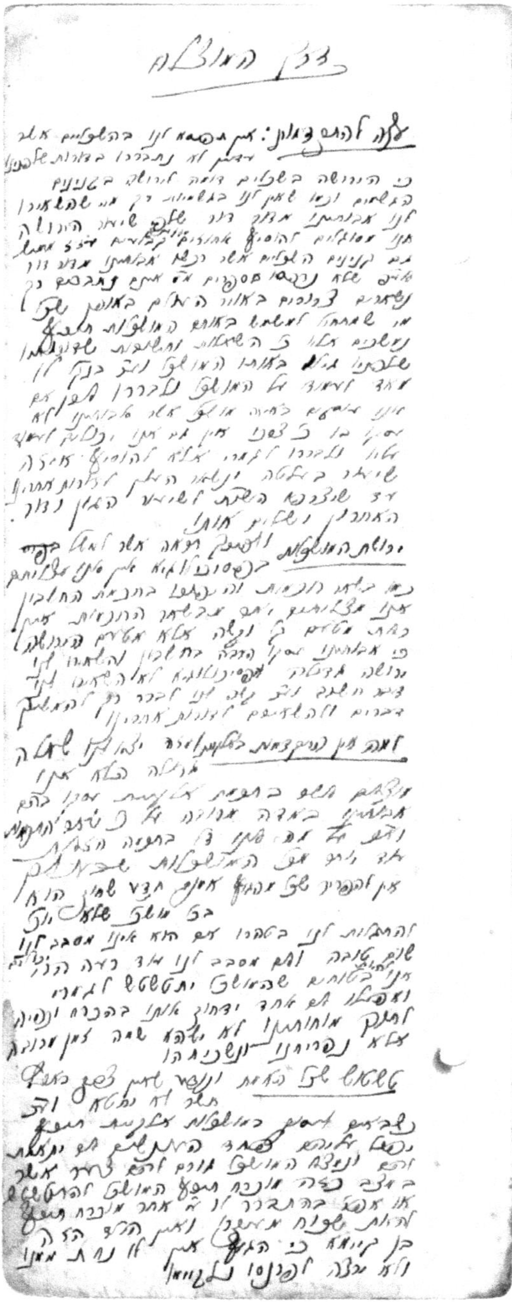

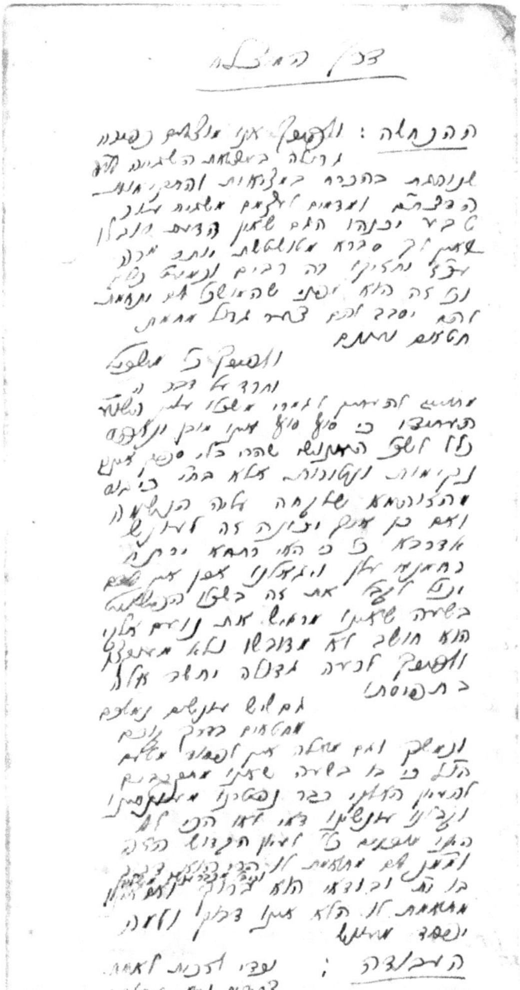

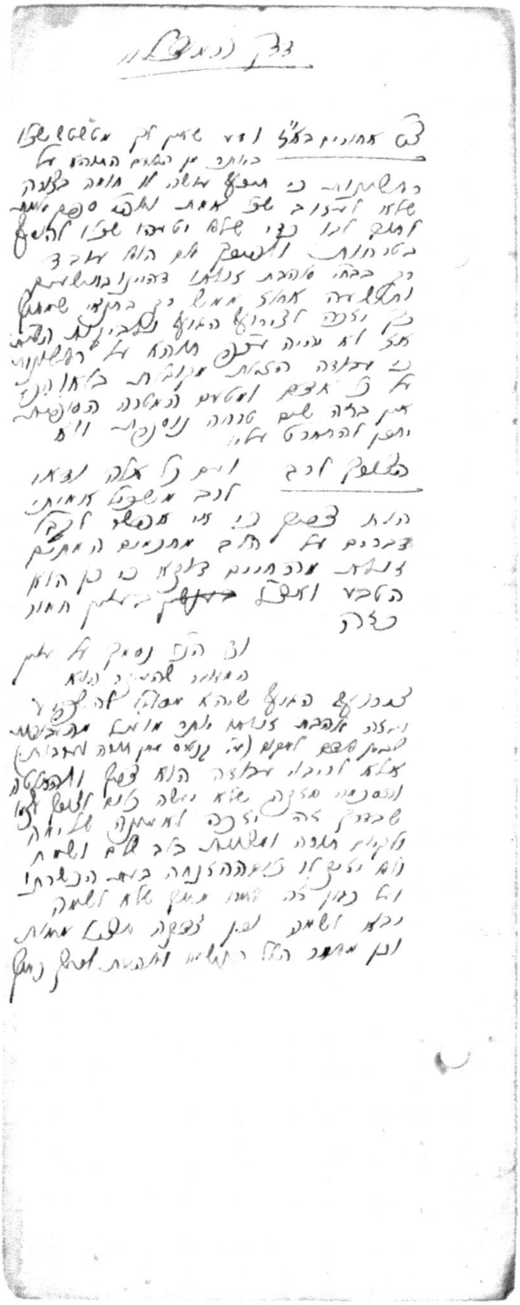

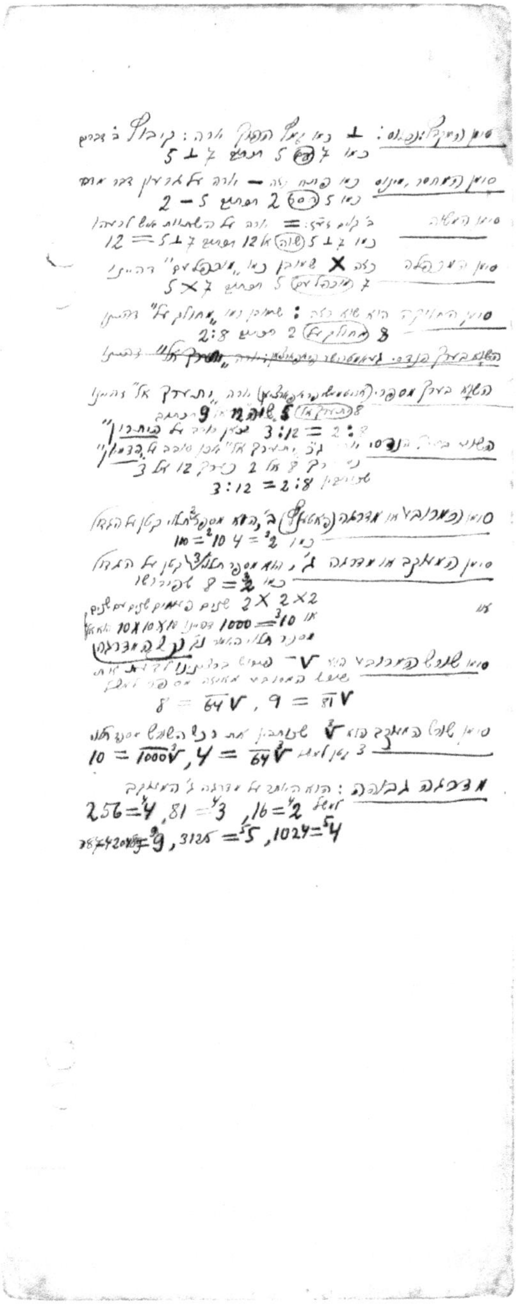

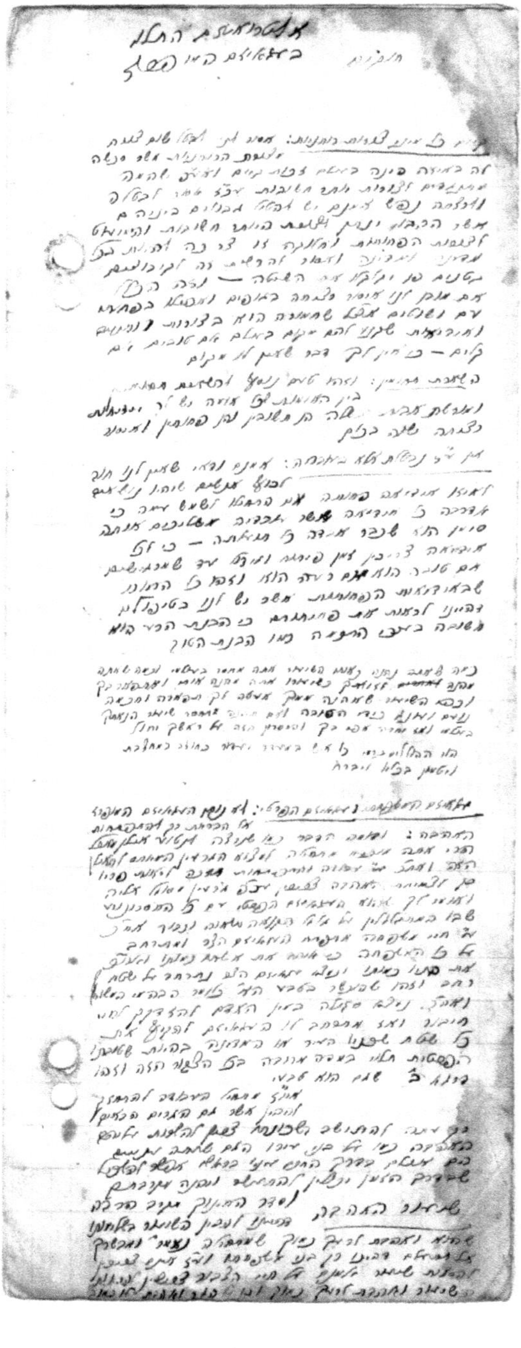

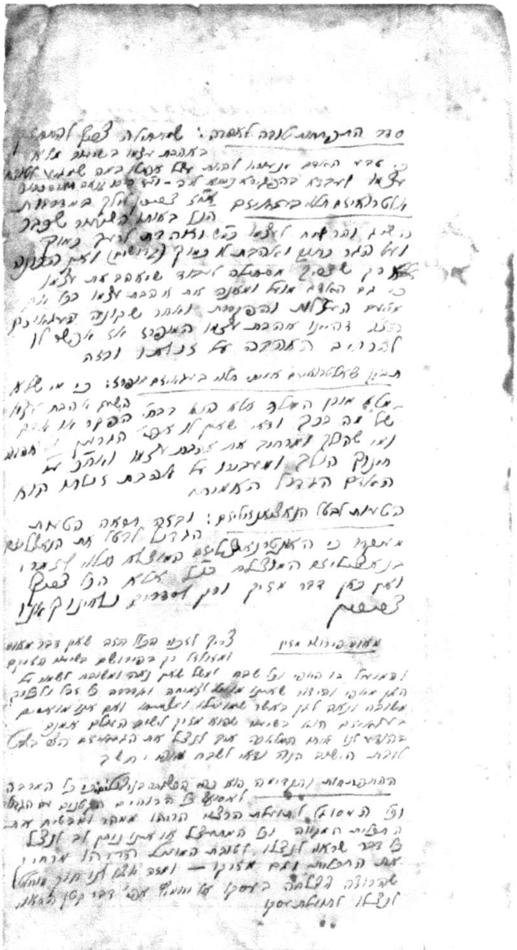

Kabbalistic Concepts

248 – There are 248 bone segments in the human body as well as 248 words in the *Shema* prayer and 248 positive Precepts (spiritual actions). These positive Precepts are proactive "do" actions, and each one relates to a different part of the body. When we perform these Precepts, we are strengthening our body.

365 – There are 365 tendons and sinews in the human body as well as 365 negative Precepts. These negative Precepts are proactive "don't do" actions, referring to acts of restriction where we refrain from acting on our negative and selfish impulses. Each Precept corresponds to a different sinew and tendon as well as to each of the 365 days of the year.

613 – The total number of Precepts we can perform to get spiritually closer to the Light of the Creator. All 613 Precepts can be found within the Five Books of Moses. They are separated into two categories: 248 positive Precepts of proactive "do" actions, and 365 negative Precepts of proactive "do not do" actions. Performing both types of Precepts will bring us closer to the Creator. See also: Precept

6000 Years of *Tikkun* – *Tikkun* means "correction," and these 6000 years began with the creation of the world and will culminate at the end of the 6th millennium. Our correction concerns the sin of Adam and Eve, who ate from the Tree of Knowledge. The Tree of Knowledge is a code for them having listened to their selfish desires. These 6000 years of *tikkun* are divided into three eras, each consisting of 2000 years.

Angel – Frequencies or clusters of spiritual energy that constantly roam and move among us, acting as messengers of the Creator and affecting things that happen in our daily life. An angel is a conduit or channel that transports cosmic energy or thoughts from one place to another or from one spiritual dimension to the other. Angels have no free choice, and each angel is dedicated to one specific purpose. See also: Other Gods

Animal Kingdom – The third of the Four Kingdoms (Inanimate, Vegetation, Animal, Speaking), with a larger capacity of a Desire to Receive than both the Inanimate and Vegetation Kingdoms, but less than the Speaking Kingdom.

Ari, The – Hebrew for the "Holy Lion," and the name given to Rav Isaac Luria, who was born in 1534 and passed away in 1572 in the city of Safed in the Galilee region of Israel. Considered to be the father of contemporary Kabbalah, the Ari was a foremost kabbalistic scholar and the founder of the Lurianic method of learning and teaching Kabbalah. His closest student, Rav Chaim Vital, compiled and wrote the Ari's teachings in 18 volumes. These 18 volumes are known collectively as the *Writings of the Ari* or *Kitvei Ari*.

Between a Person and His Friend – This is a term used when describing Precepts of the Torah that have to do with the relationship between a person and his fellow man, like "Honor your father and mother," "Do not kill," "Do not steal," "Return a lost object," etc.

Between a Person and the Creator – This is a term used when describing Precepts of the Torah that have to do with the relationship between a person and the Creator; like connecting to the energy of Holidays, meditations, etc.

***Binah* (Intelligence)** – The third of the Ten *Sefirot* (levels) that exist in each of the Four Spiritual Worlds. *Binah* is the direct channel that funnels the Light of the Creator through the other levels into our physical world. *Binah* serves as a storehouse and source of energy—physical, emotional, intellectual, and spiritual—for our whole universe.

Body – The Lower Seven *Sefirot*: *Chesed* (Mercy), *Gevurah* (Judgment/Might), *Tiferet* (Beauty), *Netzach* (Eternity/Victory), *Hod* (Glory), *Yesod* (Foundation), and *Malchut* (Kingdom). These Seven *Sefirot* are called the Body (Heb. *Guf*) because they relate to the physical manifestation of action, which is done by the body. The Upper Three *Sefirot* (*Keter, Chochmah,* and *Binah*) are called the Head because they represent the potential aspect—the thoughts and ideas.

Book of Formation (*Sefer Yetzirah*) – The earliest known book of kabbalistic knowledge and wisdom. Written by Abraham the Patriarch some 3800 years ago, it deals primarily with the intrinsic power within the Aramaic-Hebrew letters and the stars, and how they affect us in this world. All the secrets of Creation that will eventually be revealed are considered to be concealed in this book.

***Chasadim,* Light of** (Light of Mercy) – When a person awakens within him- or herself a desire for the Light of the Creator through transforming his Desire to Receive into one of Receiving for the Sake of Sharing he creates a new Light called the Light of *Chasadim* (Mercy). This Light enclothes the Light of *Chochmah* (Wisdom), which is the essence of the Light of the Creator.

***Chayah* (Life sustaining)** – The fourth part of a person's soul known as *Chayah* (Life sustaining) is very rarely connected to and awakened. When we connect with our *Chayah* it means that we have achieved an elevated level of spirituality where we no longer have the evil inclination within. *Chayah* (Life sustaining) is the Light of the *Sefirah* of *Chochmah* (Wisdom) that provides life and sustains it.

***Chesed* (Mercy)** – The fourth level of the Ten (*Sefirot*) that exist in each of the Four Spiritual Worlds. *Chesed* is comprised of Right Column energy, the positive pole of the spiritual energy, which is sharing. The Chariot (*Merkavah*) for the *Sefira* of *Chesed* is Abraham the Patriarch.

***Chochmah* (Wisdom)** – The second level of the Ten *Sefirot* that exists in each of the Four Spiritual Worlds. A level of energy where the end result of the most complicated process is known at the very beginning.

Cleaving – A concept describing absolute closeness to the Creator. In spirituality, closeness is determined not by space or distance but by Affinity or Similarity of Form. The closer we are to behaving like the Creator, the closer we get to becoming like God. When we act selfishly, reactively, negatively we distance ourselves from the Creator and cannot cleave to Him, but when we act selflessly—as the Creator—we become closer to Him.

Clothing– All spiritual energy, like the Lightforce of the Creator, needs to be concealed in order to be revealed. This concealment is referred to as clothing. Our thoughts, words, and actions are clothing for the Lightforce of the Creator. Our body is the clothing for our soul. The Torah is the clothing for the Creator. When a Vessel receives assistance from a lower Vessel then the lower one is a garment or clothing for the upper Vessel.

Concealed Torah – Aspects of the Torah whose meaning is hidden; also called the Secrets of the Torah. Concealed Torah is essentially a reference to the Wisdom of Kabbalah. One reason that Kabbalah is referred to as the Concealed Torah is because it is concealed from the immediate and literal understanding of the Torah.

Creator – The Endless Light or the Lightforce of God, the Cause of all Causes.

Days of the Messiah – Known as the 1000 Years of Peace; a time when the world and its inhabitants will experience pure happiness, pleasure, bliss, joy and fulfillment. There will be no death, no intolerance and no hatred.

Death is Eternally Swallowed – During the Days of the Messiah, there will be no more death. It will be swallowed up forever by the Light of the Creator. This also refers to the Resurrection of the Dead that will occur during this time.

Desire – A Vessel; a measurement of how much we are willing to work for and earn that which we want to have or achieve. There can be no action of any kind without some form of desire, whether conscious or subconscious.

Difference of Form – The essence of the Creator is unconditional sharing. When we act selfishly and do not share selflessly, we are in Difference of Form with the Creator. We have distanced ourselves from the Creator and thus cannot cleave to Him. It is the opposite of Similarity of Form.

***Ein Sof* (Endless)** – Before Creation all that existed was the Endless Light of the Creator. There was no lack; all desires where completely fulfilled. The Vessel—the Desire to Receive—had no blemishes of the Desire to Receive for Oneself Alone.

End [of the *Tikkun*] – When we, as a collective, transform our nature to become completely sharing beings, when we are in true Similarity of Form with the Creator, we have reached the end of the *Tikkun* (lit. fixing/correction), and the Days of the Messiah (see above) will arrive.

***Etz HaChayim* (Tree of Life)** – The first four volumes in the 18-volume set of the Writings of the Ari, written by Rav Isaac Luria (the Ari). These volumes contain the main teachings of the study of the *Ten Luminous Emanations.*

Evil Inclination – We all have two inner voices that guide us in everything we do. The evil inclination is the voice of our internal opponent that pushes us to be reactive, do selfish things and act negatively. It is sometimes referred to as Satan, which in Hebrew means "adversary."

Exile – A state of existence where we are less connected and less in tune with the Light, a state where chaos rules and miracles are rare.

Final Generation – The generation that will live in the time when world peace will prevail and humanity as a whole will have transformed into unique individuals who use their uniqueness to share with others rather than receive for oneself alone.

For Its Own Sake – Doing something just for the sake of revealing the Light without any personal agenda or ulterior thought behind it. This term is commonly said about the study of the Torah and the Precepts. In Hebrew, it is called *Lishma*.

Free will – The kabbalists explain we are born with free will and that our lives are not preordained. Free will is the ability to choose to surrender to our Desire to Receive for Oneself Alone or to transform it to the Desire to Receive for the Sake of Sharing.

***Gevurah* (Judgment/Might)** – The fifth of the ten levels (*Sefirot*) that exist in each of the Four Spiritual Worlds. *Gevurah* is comprised of Left Column energy. The Chariot for the *Sefira* of *Gevurah* is Isaac the Patriarch.

Give Pleasure to the Creator – Every spiritual action that we do For Its Own Sake—every time we change our selfish nature without any personal agenda, every time that we follow the Light without receiving anything in return—is considered to be Giving Pleasure to our Creator.

Governance of Earth – The Creator gave human beings tools to voluntarily accelerate the process of evolution and the *Tikkun* process on their own accord. See: "I will hasten it."

Governance of Heaven – The laws of spiritual nature that guide every person, creature and atom to go through its own individual evolution without necessarily being aware of this process. It is also called Providence. See: "In its time"

Gradual Evolution – The Creator did not complete the worlds that He created so as to give humanity the space to work and evolve from a state of pure ego and Desire to Receive for the Self Alone and become more God-like. This process of evolution occurs whether we are aware of it or not; and whether we actively choose to evolve or not.

Habakkuk – A prophet of the Israelites (circa 600 BCE). He is one of the 12 Minor Prophets who have a book named after them in the 24 Books of the Torah. Habakkuk died as a child and was resurrected by the prophet Elisha.

HaSulam – Literally "The Ladder." Written by Rav Yehuda Ashlag, *HaSulam* is a Hebrew translation with commentary of the Aramaic text of the *Zohar*. It is a stepping stone or ladder toward understanding the hidden secrets coded in the *Zohar*.

***Hod* (Glory)** – The eighth of the ten levels (*Sefirot*) that exist in each of the Four Spiritual Worlds. *Hod* is comprised of the energy of the Left Column, although less intense than *Gevurah*. The Chariot for the *Sefira* of *Hod* is Aaron the High Priest. See also: *Gevurah*, Lower Seven, Ten *Sefirot*.

Holiness – A term used to describe the spiritual level attained where a person is battling and resisting his ego and evil inclination and is instead sharing selflessly. This term is also used to describe items or places, and the level of connection we can make through them. For example, Jerusalem is called the Holy City because it is the energy center of the world and where we can make our strongest connection to the Creator.

"I Will Hasten It" – In the Book of Isaiah (60:22), there is a section that speaks about the days of the Final Redemption, where there will be no more war and bloodshed, chaos and suffering. If we change our selfish nature and earn this merit, then the Creator says to Isaiah, "I will hasten it"—meaning bring about the Final Redemption sooner.

Impure System –The system made up of only the Right and Left Columns, with the exclusion of the Central Column to balance the flow of Light and energy. This system creates a short circuit in our soul, which in turn fuels the negative side or Satan.

Impurity – A term used to describe the level in which a person is failing to resist his ego and evil inclination and sinking lower and lower into selfishness.

"In Its Time" – In the Book of Isaiah (60:22), there is a section that speaks about the days of the Final Redemption, where there will be no more war and bloodshed, chaos and suffering. If we have not changed our selfish nature and continue in our negative ways of life, then the Creator says to Isaiah that the Redemption will come "in its time," meaning at the end of the 6000 Years of *Tikkun*, and not sooner.

Inanimate – Of the four Kingdoms (Inanimate, Vegetation, Animal, Speaking), this is the first and lowest level, containing the lowest intensity of Desire to Receive.

Isaiah – One of the greatest prophets (circa 740 BCE) who preached for social justice based on understanding the Providence of the Creator. He urged people to reconnect to spirituality rather than dogmatic religion. Isaiah prophesized the end of days as a time when there would be peace on Earth and a reality where "a wolf shall dwell with a lamb."

Israelite – A code name for anyone following a spiritual path and working on his or her negative traits, constantly striving to transform them to positive ones. Israelites are people who take upon themselves the responsibility for spreading the Light, putting other people's needs before their own, following the spiritual rules of cause and effect, and not taking the Torah literally but rather as a coded message.

Job – A righteous man in biblical times whose piety and selflessness prompted Satan to test his virtue with terrible physical suffering, both within and without. Job never succumbed to the pain, always staying true to the Creator, and was ultimately rewarded double what he had lost. The *Book of Job* deals with the question of why good people suffer and evil people prosper.

***Keter* (Crown)** – The first and highest of the ten levels (*Sefirot*) that exist in each of the Four Spiritual Worlds. *Keter* is the ultimate connection to the Lightforce of the Creator and is the seed level of every spiritual and physical dimension.

King David – The second king of Israel (reigned circa 1010–970 BCE), but the first from the tribe of Judah. Chosen by God and anointed by the prophet Samuel, David was not only a great warrior who expanded his kingdom but also the composer of the *Book of Psalms.* King David is the Chariot of the *Sefira* of *Malchut* (Kingdom), representing the duality of the physical reality, that of fighting for survival while awakening our spiritual essence at the same time. King David is the seed of the future Messiah.

King Solomon – The son of King David and third king of Israel (reigned circa 970 – 931 BCE). King Solomon built the First Temple in Jerusalem. Known as the wisest man to ever live, mastering all aspects of wisdom in the world. His name in Hebrew, *Shlomo*, means "completion" or "wholeness" as well as "peace," and during his reign, there were no wars anywhere on the planet.

Light of the Creator –The all-encompassing energy of the Creator received in all the worlds. It is everything except the Vessel—which is the Desire to Receive.

Lower Seven – In each of the Four Spiritual Worlds there are ten levels or *Sefirot*. The Lower Seven *Sefirot* are *Chesed* (Mercy), *Gevurah* (Judgment/Might), *Tiferet* (Beauty), *Netzach* (Eternity/Victory), *Hod* (Glory), *Yesod* (Foundation), and *Malchut* (Kingdom). Collectively, the Lower Seven *Sefirot* represent the six directions: south, north, east, up, down, and west.

***Malchut* (Kingdom)** – The tenth and lowest of the ten levels (*Sefirot*) that exist in each of the Four Spiritual Worlds. *Malchut* represents manifestation and our physical world. The Chariot for the *Sefira* of *Malchut* is King David.

Merit – In Hebrew, this word is *zechut*, which is derived from the root word "pure," meaning that when we transform our selfish nature into one of selflessness and sharing with others, we become pure and thus merit our next spiritual level.

Messiah – Often described as a person, the concept of Messiah simply means a collective consciousness of humanity where everyone cares about another's needs ahead of their own, and in this way emulating the complete selflessness of the Light. All forms of death (in health, business, relationships, or anything else) cannot exist within the realm of this consciousness.

Mishnah – A six-volume explanation of the spiritual laws in the *Five Books of Moses*. Each volume deals with a specific category of law. The *Mishnah* was originally an oral teaching, passed on from teacher to student. Following the destruction of the Second Temple, Rav Yehuda HaNasi collected all the *Mishnahs* and placed them in categories in a written format. The *Mishnah* was composed by *Tanna'im*, kabbalistic sages living in Israel between the years 200 BCE to 200 CE.

Moses – Known as the greatest prophet to ever live, Moses was an intermediary for the Israelites to receive the Ten Utterances from

God at Mount Sinai. He led the Israelites through the wilderness to the bank of the Jordan River but did not enter with them into the land of Israel.

Mount Sinai Revelation – The event (circa 1300 BCE) where the Israelites, by achieving total unity, received the Torah on Mount Sinai. The Israelites experienced immortality, mind over matter, and the reality existing beyond the five senses.

Nefesh – The lowest part of our soul. It is our basal consciousness and animal instinct for survival. *Nefesh* is usually fueled by the Desire to Receive and it has two levels: Animalistic *Nefesh* which is the Desire to Receive for the Self Alone and the Spiritual *Nefesh* which is the Desire to Receive for the Sake of Sharing. Because the connection to *Nefesh* is through the blood, the Torah states that we should not eat or drink animal blood, so as not to connect to the raw animal instinct of the animal. Throughout a person's life, at certain age-related milestones, we awaken and connect to additional parts of the soul. See also: *Ruach*, *Neshamah*, *Chayah*, *Yechidah*

Neshamah **(Soul)** – The third part of our soul, which we awaken and connect to when we reach the age of 20. The *Neshamah* helps us to connect directly to the power of the Creator. It is compatible with the Light that is contained in *Binah*.

Netzach **(Eternity/Victory)** – The seventh of the ten levels (*Sefirot*) that exist in each of the Four Spiritual Worlds. *Netzach* is comprised of the energy of the Right Column, although less powerful than *Chesed*. The Chariot for the *Sefira* of *Netzach* is Moses.

Not For Its Own Sake – A concept also known as *Lo Lishma*, it refers to a spiritual action that is done with a hidden agenda, where you are trying to get something for yourself alone. See also: For Its Own Sake

Numerical Value – There are 22 Hebrew letters, each with a numerical value ranging from 1 to 400, which when combined produce words and phrases with their own unique numerical values. Words or phrases that have the same numerical value provide us with spiritual insight for our lives. The main sources for deciphering these combinations are *Sefer Yetzirah* (*Book of Formation*), the *Zohar*, and the *Writings of the Ari.*

Oral Torah – The Wisdom of the Torah that was not given to the Israelites on Mount Sinai as part of the Written Torah, but was taught orally by the Creator to Moses, who in turn transmitted it to the Israelites. This wisdom continued to be taught orally until it was eventually written down as the *Mishnah* and *Talmud.*

Other Side – The negative side, the evil inclination, the Satan.

Paradise – The 99% Realm where there is no chaos, pain or suffering, only happiness and fulfillment.

PaRDeS – Every word and letter in the Torah can be understood in four different ways: ***Peshat*** – the simple and literal meaning; ***Remez*** – the allegorical meaning behind the words, metaphors that stand for a higher meaning; ***Derash*** – the in-depth explanation and homiletical meanings; and ***Sod*** – the secrets behind the words, and where the Wisdom of Kabbalah comes from. The first letter of each creates the acronym PRDS, pronounced as ***PaRDeS,*** which means "orchard."

Partzuf – A complete spiritual structure of the Ten *Sefirot.* A *partzuf* represents the Head, the Upper Three *Sefirot*—potential; and the Lower Seven *Sefirot,* the Body—actual.

People of Construction – Are interested in supporting and upholding the community as a whole. As a result they were often forced to give up their possessions for the sake of others.

People of Destruction – Are more inclined toward lawlessness and never wanting to give up even a small part of their share for the sake of others. They do not take into account that they are endangering the existence of the community.

Peshat – The simple meaning behind the words of the Torah, the literal meaning of the stories and events. *Peshat* is considered the cornerstone for the other three ways of understanding the Torah.

Precept – One of the 613 spiritual actions we can perform to connect to the Light of the Creator. There are two types of Precepts: those between man and his fellowman, and those between man and the Creator. In Hebrew the word for Precept is *Mitzvah*, meaning "unity" or "bonding" showing us that the Precepts create unity between us and the Creator.

Primordial Man (*Adam Kadmon*) – Our soul ascends and descends through four spiritual worlds during the course of the day as we make our spiritual connections—*Atzilut* (Emanation), *Beriah* (Creation), *Yetzirah* (Formation), *Asiyah* (Action). Above these four worlds is one world that we cannot reach through our connections, known as Primordial Man. See also: World of *Atzilut* (Emanation), World of *Beriah* (Creation), World of *Yetzirah* (Formation), World of *Asiyah* (Action).

Prologue to the *Zohar* – The first volume of the *Zohar*; it contains sections of commentary that detail many esoteric concepts, which do not necessarily relate to any one portion.

Prophet – A person chosen to speak for God by Divine Inspiration and to guide the people of Israel.

Proverbs, Book of – One of the 24 Books of the Bible. The *Book of Proverbs* was written by King Solomon and deals with life lessons.

Providence – Everything that happens on this Earth is led by Divine Providence. The *Zohar* tells us that even every blade of grass has its own individual angel that tells it to grow. In short, every action or event that happens is overseen by the Creator Himself, and no matter how bad things may seem to us, the Light of Creator is there.

Psalms, Book of – One of the 24 Books of the Bible. The *Book of Psalms* was written by King David as songs and poems that teach us about life and about one's personal relationship with the Creator. Many prayers are based on Psalms, and the *Zohar* often quotes this book.

Pure – Without spiritual blemish. Someone or something that is completely clean from negativity; there is less of a Desire to Receive and more of a Desire to Share. The purer a person is, the more Light can shine through him and illuminate his life and the lives of others around him.

Rav Chaim Vital – The closest and greatest student of Rav Isaac Luria (the Ari). Blessed with an incredible memory, he was able to write everything the Ari taught him during the two years they were together before the Ari passed away, resulting in the 18-volume set of the *Writings of the Ari*. See also: Ari

Rav Elazar ben Shimon – Son of the author of the *Zohar*, the great kabbalist Rav Shimon bar Yochai. Around 2000 years ago, Rav Elazar and his father hid from the Romans in a cave for 13 years where the Wisdom of the *Zohar* was revealed to them by Moses and Elijah the Prophet.

Rav Shimon bar Yochai – the Master Kabbalist and author of the *Zohar*, the foremost work of kabbalistic knowledge. He was a *Tanna* of the second century, and student of Rabbi Akiva. He received his Divine knowledge from Moses and Elijah the prophet while hiding in a cave with his son, Rav Elazar. For Rav Shimon bar Yochai, the limitation of time, space and motion did not exist.

Receiving for the Sake of Sharing – Describes an action of receiving where the purpose is not to just receive for oneself alone, but to receive with the intention of wanting to share what is received with another.

Remez – The hidden meaning behind the words in the Torah. See also: *PaRDeS*.

Repentance (*Teshuvah*) – Meaning literally "to return," repentance should be understood as a transformation of thought or action to correct a wrong we have done. By doing so, we take responsibility and own up to our past mistakes, thereby removing whatever chaos and pain we might face as a result in the future.

Resurrection of the Dead – In the Days of Messiah, where there will be no more death, and everyone who has previously died will come back to life and be with us again. Kabbalist Rav Ashlag explains that during the time of Messiah everyone will be resurrected with their defects, with their selfish natures and characteristics, and will be given the opportunity to transform these defects and make themselves pure.

Revealed Torah – The written Torah, *Mishnah*, and *Talmud*.

Revealed Wisdom – Any part of the Wisdom of Kabbalah whose meaning is accessible and easy to understand.

Reward and Punishment – Code words for the basic universal law of cause and effect. The Creator does not punish or reward us for our behavior. Our actions simply create an effect or consequence that comes back to us in the same degree, good or bad, depending on whether our action was positive or negative.

Righteous (*Tzadik*) – A person who is completely devoted to working on transforming his or her negative traits and to sharing unconditionally with others. The *Midrash* tells us that a righteous person is someone whose positive actions outweigh his or her negative actions.

Rishonim (lit. the Firsts) – The great commentators on the *Mishnah* and *Talmud* who lived between the 11th and 15th centuries CE. Two of the most prominent *Rishonim* are *Rashi* and the *Tosefot.*

Root – As creations of God, we can be likened to branches on a tree, whereas the Creator is the root that gives the branches life.

Ruach – Of the five levels that make up the soul, *Ruach*, which means "Spirit," is the second level above the *Nefesh*. It is the part of our soul that is awakened when we reach Bar/Bat Mitzvah (age 13 for a boy, 12 for a girl), activating our free will to choose between Light and darkness, good and bad.

Sages – A term used to refer to kabbalists from the time of the Second Temple. These were all very wise men who left us with deep wisdom and many lessons to be found in the *Mishnah,* the *Talmud*, and the *Zohar*.

Shells (*Klippot*) – Evil husks created by mankind's negative deeds. It is a metaphysical negative covering that hides the Light of the Creator from us and gives it to the Negative Side. The Shells also latch on to the sparks of Light we are not able to elevate when we fail to act on a positive impulse or action, or when we perform a selfish or negative action.

Similarity of Form – Describes how close we are to the Creator. The essence of the Creator is unconditional sharing. When we act selflessly and do not receive selfishly, we are in Similarity of Form with the Creator. We can cleave to Him, getting closer to His Supernal Splendor.

Sitrei Torah – The concealed Wisdom of Kabbalah and the Torah. All secrets and teachings of Kabbalah and the Torah can be divided into two categories: *Sitrei Torah* (Secrets of the Torah) and *Ta'amei Torah* (Taste or Meaning of the Torah). *Sitrei Torah* can only be revealed to someone who merits and has earned Divine revelation through a teacher, an angel or Elijah the Prophet. See also: *Ta'amei Torah.*

Sod – One of the four ways to interpret every word and sentence in the Torah. *Sod* is the Secrets of the Torah, the Wisdom of Kabbalah. See also: *PARDES*

Speaking – There are four Kingdoms (Inanimate, Vegetation, Animal and Speaking) that describe levels of consciousness as well as indicate the intensity of each Kingdom's Desire to Receive. Humans have the greatest Desire to Receive of any creation, and are unique in that they can use the power of the spoken word to both create and destroy. This is the highest level of Desire out of the four Kingdoms.

Surrounding Light – A term used in the study of the *Ten Luminous Emanations*. There are two forms of Light: the Inner Light – the Light that we reveal by our actions; and the Surrounding Light – the rest of the Light that has the potential to be revealed in our life. This Surrounding Light pushes us to grow and reveal this potential Light.

Ta'amei Torah – Literally "Taste or Meaning of the Torah." The revealed wisdom of Kabbalah and the Torah. *Ta'amei Torah* refers to the teachings of the Torah that have a clear and understandable explanation for each connection we make in our daily life through studying and performing the Precepts. These teachings are usually not concealed and are made known to everyone.

Talmud – A written compendium of the explanations and commentaries by sages of the 3rd to 7th centuries CE on the laws in the *Five Books of Moses* regarding ethics, customs, and history. It includes the *Mishnah*, the *Gemarah*, and the *Tosefot*, as well as commentaries by *Rashi* and many other commentators. There are two *Talmuds*: The *Babylonian Talmud* and the *Jerusalem Talmud*. After the destruction of the Temple, many sages were exiled in Babylon, hence the *Babylonian Talmud*.

Ten *Sefirot* – The ten levels of consciousness present in each of the Four Spiritual Worlds. The Ten *Sefirot* Are: *Keter* (Crown), *Chochmah* (Wisdom), *Binah* (Intelligence), *Chesed* (Mercy), *Gevurah* (Judgment/Might), *Tiferet* (Beauty), *Netzach* (Eternity/Victory), *Hod* (Glory), *Yesod* (Foundation), and *Malchut* (Kingdom). They are ten Vessels that reveal the Light; the greater the desire, the higher the level of consciousness that is revealed.

Ten Luminous Emanations – The study of the emanations of the *Sefirot* from the Endless down to our physical world, compiled into seven volumes. Written by Rav Yehuda Ashlag, founder of The Kabbalah Centre, this study is vital for any deep understanding of the *Zohar* and the way our universe functions.

Tetragrammaton – The four-letter combination of the Name of God, spelled out with the letters *Yud* and *Hei* and *Vav* and *Hei*. This is the Name of God that denotes absolute mercy and sharing.

This World – The physical world we live in where we are subject to the laws of cause and effect and bound by the limitations of time, space, and motion. Also called the 1% Reality and the Illusionary World.

Tiferet (Beauty) – The sixth of the ten levels (*Sefirot*) that exist in each of the Four Spiritual Worlds. *Tiferet* comprises the Central Column, since this *Sefira* is found between *Chesed* (Right Column) and *Gevurah* (Left Column). The Chariot for the *Sefira* of *Tiferet* is Jacob the Patriarch.

Tikkun (Correction) – We come to this world to correct the selfish aspects of our nature and to transform ourselves into beings of sharing. Everything we experience in life—good or bad—is a *Tikkun* process by which we correct, cleanse, and elevate our souls. The purpose of *Tikkun* is to bring every human being, along with the entire universe, to perfection. Also known as karma and the purpose of reincarnation.

Tikkunei HaZohar – Literally "Corrections to the *Zohar*," written as 72 commentaries on the first word of Genesis (*Beresheet*). *Tikkunei HaZohar* discourses upon teachings specifically directed to the Age of Aquarius. This is the first instruction that Rav Shimon bar Yochai received in the cave.

Torah – The *Five Books of Moses*. The entire body of biblical study, including the *Five Books of Moses*, the 24 other Books of the Bible, the *Mishnah*, the *Talmud*, and Kabbalah, can also be referred to as *Torah*.

Tractate – The *Talmud* and *Mishnah* are each split into six sections, each of which is further divided into subsections called *Masechet* or *Tractates*. Each subsection is given a name to describe the topic of discussion.

Tractate *Avot* (Fathers) – Also known as *Pirkei Avot* (Lessons of Our Fathers), this is one of a very few Tractates in the *Mishnah* that does not have a *Gemarah* commentary on it. This Tractate consists of ethical moral principles and wise sayings to live by.

Tractate *Berachot* (Blessings) – This Tractate discusses the prayers we say every day as well as the blessings we say throughout the day over food and drink.

Tractate *Ta'anit* (Fasting) – This Tractate discusses the laws of fast days and the proceedings and prayers involved.

Transgression – Also referred to as sin or iniquity. These are all code words for one thing: a disconnection from the Light of the Creator and a connection to darkness, chaos, pain, and suffering.

Tree of Knowledge – The Tree of Knowledge Good and Evil that is mentioned in the Torah is a metaphor for connecting to the physical reality and our ego, where we are limited by our five senses. It affords us the opportunity to exercise our free will to choose between good and bad, the Light or our selfish behaviors.
Tree of Life – The Tree of Life mentioned in the Torah is a metaphor for the Flawless Universe beyond our 1% physical reality.

Tzimtzum **(Contraction)** –The Vessel's voluntary rejection or restriction of the Divine Light in the Endless World due to the concept of Bread of Shame and the Vessel's desire to be independent and God-like. In the lower physical world the restriction, if not done voluntarily, is imposed.

Unique Individuality – our soul is a spark extended directly from the Creator who is one, only and unique. We are carrying the same spiritual DNA and naturally feel one, only and unique. Each and every one of us feels that the world was created just for him or her and that the whole world is there to serve the "me": This law of unique individuality should neither be condemned nor praised. It is what it is and as such it is an absolute truth.

Upper Three – The term used to refer to the first three *Sefirot*: *Keter* (Crown), *Chochmah* (Wisdom), and *Binah* (Intelligence). Out of the Ten *Sefirot*, these three are on the highest plane of existence.

Vegetation – Of the four Kingdoms (Inanimate, Vegetation, Animal, Speaking), this is the second level, with a more intense Desire to Receive than the Inanimate Kingdom, but less than Animal and Speaking Kingdoms.

Vessel – The Desire to Receive that exists in all things of Creation.

Wisdom of Truth – Another term for the Wisdom of Kabbalah, so called because truth is something that is neither subjective nor inconsistent. Truth is a constant and does not change because of human influences.

Worlds (*Olamot*) – A term used in the study of the *Ten Luminous Emanations*. There are five channels that bring the Light down to this mundane reality. When the channels are filled with Light we call them Worlds. Every World represents a different level of consciousness that is related to a level of veil that covers the Light. The word *olam* in Hebrew means "disappearance," referring to the fact that only when the Light is concealed can a reality be revealed. The Worlds are: Primordial Man (*Adam Kadmon*), Emanation (*Atzilut*), Creation (*Beriah*), Formation (*Yetzirah*), and Action (*Asiyah*).

Worlds of Holiness – The worlds governed by the Endless Light: *Adam Kadmon* (Primordial Man), *Atzilut* (Emanation), *Beriah* (Creation), *Yetzirah* (Formation), *Asiyah* (Action).

Worlds of Impurity – The negative reality governed by Satan, and the opposite or mirror image of the Worlds of Holiness.

World of Action (*Asiyah*) – The lowest (from above downwards) of the Five Spiritual Worlds that emerged after the *Tzimtzum* (Contraction) of the Vessel in the Endless. The World of Action is the dimension where the least amount of Light is revealed, enabling humanity to exercise their free will in discerning between good and evil. The World of Action is also related to the *Sefira* of *Malchut* (Kingdom) and is referred to as the Tree of Knowledge of Good and Evil.

World of Creation (*Beriah*) – The third (from above downwards) of the Five Spiritual Worlds that appeared after the *Tzimtzum* (Contraction). It is related to the *Sefira* of *Binah* (Intelligence) and is humanity's universal energy store.

World of Emanation (*Atzilut*) – The second (from above downwards) of the Five Spiritual Worlds that appeared after the *Tzimtzum* (Contraction). In this high and most exalted World, the Vessel is passive in relation to the Light, allowing the Light to flow without any agenda. It is related to the *Sefira* of *Chochmah* (Wisdom).

World of Formation (*Yetzirah*) – The fourth (from above downwards) of the Five Spiritual Worlds that appeared after the *Tzimtzum* (Contraction). Whereas in the lowest World (Action), evil is the predominant force, in the World of Formation, goodness is the predominant force. It is related to the *Sefira* of *Zeir Anpin* (Small Face) and to the energy of the Shield of David.

World to Come – The realm where only happiness, fulfillment, love, and joy exist; the 99% Realm of the Light of the Creator. The kabbalists explain that the World to Come exists in each and every moment of our lives. Every action of ours creates an effect that comes back to us either for good and for bad, and through the way in which we live our lives, we can create worlds according to our design. See also: This World

Work of the Creator – Fulfilling the Precepts of the Bible and following the path of the Creator.

Written Torah – The *Five Books of Moses* and all the teachings found within that were given to the Israelites on Mount Sinai.

Yechidah (**Oneness**) – The fifth and final part of a person's soul, when he or she unifies completely with the Light of the Creator.

***Yesod* (Foundation)** – The ninth of the ten levels (*Sefirot*) that exist in each of the Four Spiritual Worlds. *Yesod* is the ultimate representation of sustenance and abundance. The Chariot for the *Sefira* of *Yesod* is Joseph the Righteous, who provided sustenance and abundance from Egypt to the whole world during a famine, as described in the Book of Genesis.

Zohar – Written by the great sage Rav Shimon bar Yochai, this 23-volume work is the basis and source of all the teachings of Kabbalah we have today.

More Ways to Bring the Wisdom of Kabbalah into your Life

The Wisdom of Truth: 12 Essays by the Holy Kabbalist Rav Yehuda Ashlag
Edited by Michael Berg

All of the essential truths of Kabbalah are encapsulated in these thought-provoking essays by arguably the most profound mystic of the 20th century. Originally published in 1984 as Kabbalah: A Gift of the Bible, and long out of print, this is a new translation from the Hebrew, edited and with an introduction by noted Kabbalah scholar Michael Berg.

And You Shall Choose Life: An Essay on Kabbalah, The Purpose of Life, and Our True Spiritual Work
By Rav Ashlag, Edited by Michael Berg

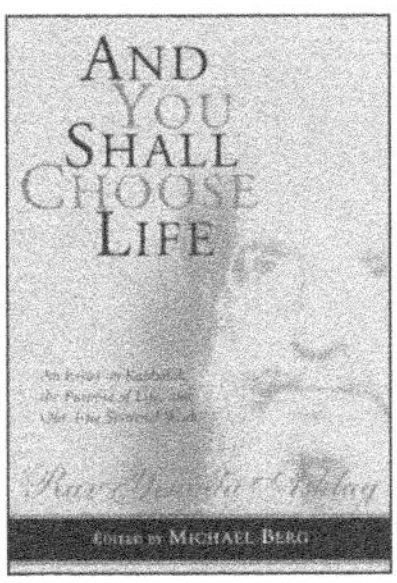

Preceding the time this essay was written in 1933-34, Kabbalah was considered taboo. But Rav Ashlag, the founder of The Kabbalah Centre, was a visionary pioneer. This book gives insight into one of the greatest kabbalistic thought leaders of all time. One of the most challenging aspects is the tone of urgency. As people were swept up in pain and suffering, Rav Ashlag tried to explain that despite outer events, the Creator is good. "Choosing life" means forming a connection to God, removing ego and pursuing the spiritual path of Kabbalah. Although written many decades ago, the essays are timeless.

The *Zohar*

The Zohar, the basic source of the Kabbalah, was authored two thousand years ago by Rabbi Shimon bar Yochai while hiding from the Romans in a cave in Peki'in for 13 years. It was later brought to light by Rabbi Moses de Leon in Spain, and further revealed through the Safed Kabbalists and the Lurianic system of Kabbalah.

The programs of The Kabbalah Centre have been established to provide opportunities for learning, teaching, research, and demonstration of specialized knowledge drawn from the ageless wisdom of the Zohar and the Jewish sages. Long kept from the masses, today this knowledge of the Zohar and Kabbalah should be shared by all who seek to understand the deeper meaning of this spiritual heritage, and a deeper and more profound meaning of life. Modern science is only beginning to discover what our sages veiled in symbolism. This knowledge is of a very practical nature and can be applied daily for the betterment of our lives and of humankind.

Darkness cannot prevail in the presence of Light. Even a darkened room must respond to the lighting of a candle. As we share this moment together we are beginning to witness, and indeed some of us are already participating in, a people's revolution of enlightenment. The darkened clouds of strife and conflict will make their presence felt only as long as the Eternal Light remains concealed. The Zohar now remains an instrument to infuse the cosmos with the revealed Lightforce of the Creator. The Zohar is not a book about religion. Rather, the Zohar is concerned with the relationship between the unseen forces of the cosmos, the Lightforce, and the impact on humanity.

The Zohar promises that with the ushering in of the Age of Aquarius, the cosmos will become readily accessible to human understanding. It states that in the days of the Messiah "there will no longer be the necessity for one to request of his neighbor, teach me wisdom." (Zohar, Naso 9:65) "One day, they will no longer teach every man his neighbor and every man his brother, saying know the Lord. For they shall all know Me, from the youngest to the oldest of them. (Jeremiah 31:34) We can regain dominion of our lives and environment. To achieve this objective, the Zohar provides us with an opportunity to transcend the crushing weight of universal negativity.

The daily perusing of the Zohar, without any attempt at translation or understanding will fill our consciousness with the Light, improving our well-being, and influencing all in our environment toward positive attitudes. Even the scanning of the Zohar by those unfamiliar with the Hebrew Alef Bet will accomplish the same result.

The connection that we establish through scanning the Zohar is one of unity with the Light of the Creator. The letters, even if we do not consciously know Hebrew or Aramaic, are the channels through which the connection is made and can be likened to dialing a telephone number or typing in the codes to run a computer program. The connection is established at the metaphysical level of our being and radiates into our physical plane of existence. But first there is the prerequisite of metaphysical "fixing." We have to consciously, through positive thought and actions, permit the immense power of the Zohar to radiate love, harmony, and peace into our lives for us to share with all humanity and the universe.

As we enter the years ahead, the Zohar will continue to be a people's book, striking a sympathetic chord in the hearts and minds of those who long for peace, truth, and relief from suffering. In the face of crises and catastrophe, the Zohar has the ability to resolve agonizing human afflictions by restoring each individual's relationship with the Lightforce of the Creator.

—Rav Berg, 1984

About the Centres

Below is a statement written by Rav Berg in 1984. It remains true today.

Through the ultimate knowledge and mystical practices of Kabbalah, one can reach the highest spiritual levels attainable. Although many people rely on belief, faith, and dogmas in pursuing the meaning of life, Kabbalists seek a spiritual connection with the Creator and the forces of the Creator, so that the strange becomes familiar, and faith becomes knowledge.

Throughout history, those who knew and practiced the Kabbalah were extremely careful in their dissemination of the knowledge because they knew the masses of mankind had not yet prepared for the ultimate truth of existence. Today, kabbalists know that it is not only proper but necessary to make the Kabbalah available to all who seek it.

The Kabbalah Centre is an independent, non-profit institute founded in Israel in 1922. The Centre provides research, information, and assistance to those who seek the insights of Kabbalah. The Centre offers public lectures, classes, seminars, and excursions to mystical sites at branches in Israel and in the United States. Branches have been opened in Mexico, Montreal, Toronto, Paris, Hong Kong, and Taiwan.

Our courses and materials deal with the Zoharic understanding of each weekly portion of the Torah. Every facet of life is covered and other dimensions, hithertofore unknown, provide a deeper connection to a superior reality. Three important beginner courses cover such aspects as: Time, Space and Motion; Reincarnation, Marriage, Divorce; Kabbalistic Meditation; Limitation of the Five Senses; Illusion-Reality; Four Phases; Male and Female, Death, Sleep, Dreams; Food; and Shabbat.

Thousands of people have benefited from the Centre's activities, and the Centre's publishing of kabbalistic material continues to be the most comprehensive of its kind in the world, including translations in English, Hebrew, Russian, German, Portuguese, French, Spanish, Farsi (Persian).

Kabbalah can provide one with the true meaning of their being and the knowledge necessary for their ultimate benefit. It can show one spirituality that is beyond belief. The Kabbalah Centre will continue to make available the Kabbalah to all those who seek it.

—Rav Berg, 1984

Born in Poland in 1886, Kabbalist Rav Yehuda Ashlag is revered by students of Kabbalah as one of the most profound mystics and spiritual teachers of the 20th Century. Among his many accomplishments was the first-ever translation of the Zohar from its original Aramaic into Hebrew.

Rav Ashlag felt a powerful need to reveal the wisdom of Kabbalah to the masses, which had previously been prohibited. This desire led him to found The Kabbalah Centre in Jerusalem in 1922, making the wisdom widely available for the first time, and thus passing on a legacy that continues to this day through Kabbalah Centre International, its teachers and students worldwide. He was the teacher and spiritual master of Rav Yehuda Brandwein, to whom leadership of The Centre was passed when Rav Ashlag died in 1954. In turn, when Rav Brandwein died in 1969, he designated Kabbalist Rav Berg to lead The Centre.

Michael Berg, son of Rav and Karen Berg and an accomplished Kabbalah scholar and teacher, was the first person to translate the entire 23-volume Zohar from ancient Aramaic into English. He began this monumental task when he was only 18 years old, and completed it ten years later. He is co-director of Kabbalah Centre International and Kabbalah University (www.ukabbalah.com), the leading educational organization and web site dedicated to the wisdom of Kabbalah. His other books include The Secret, Secrets of the Zohar, Becoming Like God, and the national bestseller, The Way. He lives in Los Angeles with his wife and three children.

www.ingramcontent.com/pod-product-compliance
Lightning Source LLC
Chambersburg PA
CBHW020442100426
42812CB00036B/3414/J
* 9 7 8 1 5 7 1 8 9 8 7 1 5 *